# APPALACHIAN TRAIL

# Data Book

## 2026

APPALACHIAN TRAIL

# Data Book

2026

Appalachian Trail Conservancy

Edited by Daniel D. Chazin

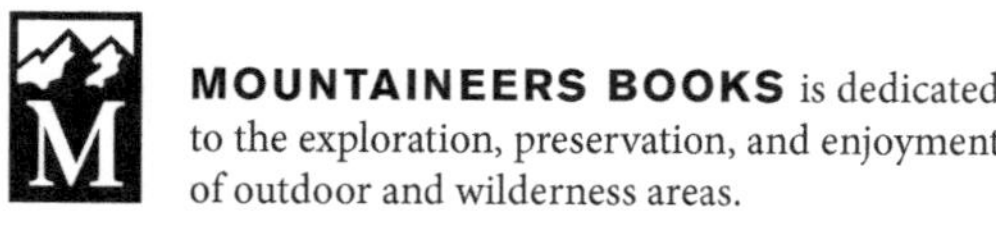

**MOUNTAINEERS BOOKS** is dedicated to the exploration, preservation, and enjoyment of outdoor and wilderness areas.

1001 SW Klickitat Way, Suite 201, Seattle, WA 98134
800-553-4453, www.mountaineersbooks.org



Printed in the United States of America
Forty-eighth edition, 2026

Cover photograph: *Franconia Ridge, New Hampshire* (Photo by Katherine Dellinger)

Leave No Trace Seven Principles © Leave No Trace, www.LNT.org

Mountaineers Books titles may be purchased for corporate, educational, or other promotional sales, and our authors are available for a wide range of events. For information on special discounts or booking an author, contact our customer service at 800-553-4453 or mbooks@mountaineersbooks.org.

Printed on FSC®-certified materials

ISBN (paperback): 978-1-68051-824-5

***An independent nonprofit publisher since 1960***

# Contents

# Introduction

There are few things more rewarding than hiking the Appalachian Trail, whether you plan to spend a couple of hours outdoors or are a Trail-tested veteran planning a thru-hike.

This *Data Book* provides a ready reference for hikers to the major features of the Appalachian Trail as it winds for more than 2,197 miles from Maine to Georgia. Many hikers find it indispensable to their journeys on the A.T. and save each year's edition with a record of their experiences and accomplishments.

The features listed here include shelters and campsites, road crossings, sources of water, elevations, principal mountain peaks and gaps, and other notable physical landmarks of America's foremost national scenic trail. Locations of areas where lodging, meals, groceries, and post offices are available are also listed, with distances and directions. Additionally, each section is marked with the Trail Club that maintains that segment; Club websites are listed on page 93.

The *Data Book* is intended to be useful in broad-scale planning of a trip of any length on the Trail, from home or while on the footpath itself. The *Data Book* does not, however, include sufficient detail for careful, complete planning of a trip. Potential hikers are encouraged to also purchase the official *Appalachian Trail Guide* books and map sets for the state(s) they plan to hike or the *Appalachian Trail Thru-Hikers' Companion.* The guidebooks contain detailed descriptions of Trail sections, facilities near the Trail, points of interest off the Trail, background on the history and natural features of the area, and other important information.

The annual compilation of each edition of the *Data Book* takes into account relocations and updated measurements that have occurred since the previous edition. That information is supplied by Appalachian Trail Conservancy staff and Trail Club volunteers who, along with land management partners, keep the Trail alive.

Keep in mind, however, that it is impossible to ensure absolute accuracy of the information in the *Data Book*, and changes will likely occur during the year of this edition. Trail-enhancing relocations that affect distances between major features are underway in some states. Also, severe weather conditions, fires, and other unpredictable developments might force temporary closings of a section. In September 2024, Hurricane Helene inflicted severe damage on the Trail in Virginia, Tennessee, and North Carolina, and repair work is still underway. A detour at Iron

Mountain Gap will be in place for at least part of 2026, and the road bridge at the Nolichucky River will take several years to rebuild.

Always check appalachiantrail.org/updates before you go for the latest Trail information conditions, and closures.

To order *Appalachian Trail Guides*, maps, the *Appalachian Trail Thru-Hiker's Companion*, and other ATC publications, go to www.mountaineersbooks.org, or call 800-553-4453. Guides to Maryland/Northern Virginia and Shenandoah National Park can be ordered at www.patc.net. The Pennsylvania guide and maps can be ordered at www.kta-hike.org.

Because maintenance of the Trail is conducted by volunteers and maintaining clubs listed in the appropriate guidebooks, questions about the exact route of the Trail should be addressed to the maintaining clubs or the Appalachian Trail Conservancy (304-535-6331; info@appalachiantrail.org).

Hikers finding errors or omissions in the *Data Book* are urged to report them by e-mail to info@appalachiantrail.org, or by mail to Data Book Editor, Appalachian Trail Conservancy, P.O. Box 807, Harpers Ferry, WV 25425. Confirmed changes will be included in the next edition.

# Safety and Ethics

Being informed and prepared is the best way to ensure your experience on the A.T. is safe and enjoyable. And being a considerate Trail user ensures that the people around you can enjoy their hike and local plants and animals can continue to thrive.

On the Trail, always carefully follow the painted white blazes and directional signs. Other key safety considerations to keep in mind are water, bear safety, and personal safety.

## WATER

Regardless of your skill, it is extremely important to plan your hike, especially in places where water is scarce. ATC and Trail Clubs attempt to locate good sources of water along the Trail but have no control over those sources and cannot, in any sense, be responsible for the quality of the water at any given time. You should ensure the safety of all water you use by purifying water drawn from any source.

## FOOD AND BEARS

ATC advocates strongly that backpackers carrying food use a hard-sided bear canister along the entire Appalachian Trail instead of attempting to use a food hang. This is because food hangs are difficult to properly do, and many are easily defeated by bears. Use provided food storage devices where available (bear boxes, cables, etc.). Hikers are required to use the bear cables in the Great Smoky Mountains National Park, regardless of which food storage method they use. See appalachiantrail.org/bears for more information about proper food storage and bear safety, as well as how to report unusual or concerning bear encounters.

## PERSONAL SAFETY

Although the Appalachian Trail is safer than most places, you should be aware that problems do occur, and a few violent crimes have occurred during the past five decades. Situational awareness is one of your best lines of defense. Be aware of what you are doing, where you are, to whom you are talking, and trust your gut. Be prudent and cautious without allowing common sense to slip into paranoia.

Here are some suggestions:

**Use extra caution if hiking alone.** If you are by yourself and encounter a stranger who makes you feel uncomfortable, say you are with a group that is behind you. Be creative. If in doubt, move on.

**Leave your hiking itinerary and timetable with someone at home.** Be sure they know your Trail name, if you have one. Check in regularly and establish a procedure to follow if you fail to check in. It helps to register your hike at atcamp.org, in case a family member needs to reach you during an extended hike. However, *do not broadcast your itinerary or location in real time* on blogs or social media.

**Be wary of strangers.** Be friendly, but cautious. Don't tell strangers about your plans. Avoid people who act suspiciously, hostile, or intoxicated.

**Don't camp near road crossings.** You're less exposed to potential negative interactions if you camp deeper in the woods among your fellow hikers.

**Leave firearms at home.** Although it is now legal to carry (but not discharge) on National Park Service lands and in most other areas with the proper state-by-state permits, firearms could be turned against you, you face a high risk of an accidental shooting, and they are extra weight.

**Eliminate opportunities for theft.** Don't bring jewelry or other valuables and keep your money hidden. If you must leave your pack, hide it carefully or leave it with someone trustworthy. Don't leave valuables or equipment (especially in sight) in vehicles parked at trailheads.

**Use the Trail and shelter registers.** Sign in, leave a note, and report any suspicious activities. If someone needs to locate you, or if a serious crime has been committed along the Trail, the first place authorities will look is in the registers.

**Report any crime or harassment.** Submit a report to the local law enforcement authorities. Once reported to local law enforcement, also submit a report to ATC by visiting appalachiantrail.org/incidents or by sending a detailed email of the incident to incidents@appalachiantrail.org. Note that submitting a report does not trigger an immediate law enforcement response.

**Report Trail emergencies.** For emergencies where you need an immediate response, call 911. Leave the Trail at the nearest road crossing and find a telephone or cell phone reception. Know your location and the location of the incident as precisely as possible. Do not use social media for emergencies.

More detailed advice is available at appalachiantrail.org/safety.

## LEAVE NO TRACE

The Appalachian Trail Conservancy, in partnership with the Leave No Trace Center for Outdoor Ethics, asks you to help take care of the Appalachian Trail and the wild country it passes through. Please do your part by following the seven Leave No Trace© principles while on the Trail:

1. Plan ahead and prepare.
2. Travel and camp on durable surfaces.
3. Dispose of waste properly.
4. Leave what you find.
5. Minimize campfire impacts.
6. Respect wildlife.
7. Be considerate of other visitors.

The continued existence of the Trail relies on each hiker being a good steward of this special place. Care should be taken not to damage the footpath itself, natural features alongside it, or the property of others through littering or other vandalism, improper fires, or use of vehicles. The needs of other users should always be considered, and special regulations must be followed in many areas. Keep day-hiking groups to 25 people or fewer and overnight groups to no more than 10 people, including leaders. Learn more at appalachiantrail.org/LNT.

Public lands are shared by all, and regulations are in place to protect sensitive areas. Please take care to learn and respect local regulations along the Trail. For example, camping permits are required in Great Smoky Mountains National Park and Shenandoah National Park. On many other parts of the Trail, camping is permitted only in designated areas. Consult the guidebooks and maps and watch for special signs along the Trail. Visit appalachiantrail.org/camping for more information.

We are all stewards of the Appalachian Trail. By practicing Leave No Trace and respecting local regulation, you can help ensure the Trail remains open and beautiful for generations to come.

## A NOTE ABOUT SAFETY

Safety is an important concern in all outdoor activities. No guidebook can alert you to every hazard or anticipate the limitations of every reader. Therefore, the descriptions of roads, trails, routes, and natural features in this book are not representations that a particular place or excursion will be safe for your party. When you follow any of the routes described in this book, you assume responsibility for your own safety. Under normal conditions, such excursions require the usual attention to traffic, road and trail conditions, weather, terrain, the capabilities of your party, and other factors. Changes resulting from maintenance work, storms, and trail relocations are constantly occurring on the Appalachian Trail so be sure to consult appalachiantrail.org/updates before you go. Always check for current conditions, obey posted private property signs, and avoid confrontations with property owners or managers. Keeping informed on current conditions and exercising common sense are the keys to a safe, enjoyable outing.

—*Mountaineers Books*

# How to Use the *Data Book*

The *Data Book* is divided into twelve chapters, beginning with Maine at Katahdin and ending with the Approach Trail to Springer Mountain in Georgia. With one exception, each chapter corresponds to a volume in the current series of *Appalachian Trail Guides*. The section beginning on page 34, for example, matches the third volume in the guidebook series, which covers the Trail in Massachusetts–Connecticut. The exception is the Trail route through the Great Smoky Mountains of Tennessee and North Carolina, which is covered in both the Tennessee–North Carolina and North Carolina–Georgia guidebooks. It is included here only in the Tennessee–North Carolina chapter. Other information is listed as follows:

**Trail Clubs** are listed in the outside margins next to the section(s) of Trail that each club maintains. The beginning and ending points of each club's range are indicated by a small gray rectangle. Website information for the clubs may be found on page 93.

**Trail sections,** as numbered and identified in the corresponding guide, are given in the columns to the left on each page, under the heading **GBS** (guidebook section). Sections are numbered consecutively, from north to south, within each state.

In the right column, under the **Map** heading, the number of the map that covers the area is listed. For more detail about a particular feature or section of the Trail, consult the relevant guidebook section or map.

**Distance from north to south** is noted for each landmark (Feature). The number is the distance, in miles, of the feature from the northern end of the part of the Trail covered in that specific chapter (read down). The number to the right of the Features and Facilities columns is the feature's distance from the **southern** end of the part of the Trail covered by this chapter (read up). The starting point for the cumulative distance is given at the top of the column.

| | | | |
|---|---|---|---|
| 0.0 | Katahdin (Baxter Peak) (5,268') | | 282.0 |
| 1.0 | Thoreau Spring | w | 281.0 |

Sometimes the Trail follows a road, ridgeline, lake, creek, or other physical feature for some distance. In those cases, usually only one distance is listed. For roads, this is generally the point at which the Trail first reaches the road proceeding from north to south, or, in some cases, the point representing the end of the section. For ridgelines, this is the highest point. Again, for more complete information about a particular feature, please consult the guidebooks, maps, or both.

**Features** include significant landmarks, roads, shelters, and other notable locations. Each section contains a list of features along or near the Trail. Towns with post offices (P.O.) are printed in boldface and carry their zip code in the listing. (i.e. **Greenwood Lake, NY, P.O. 10925**) Towns without post offices or with a post office that is far away from the Trail are listed only if the Trail goes directly through them; "P.O." is omitted in those cases.

The **elevations** of selected points along the Trail follow the name of the feature. [ i.e. Rainbow Ledges (1,517')] Those elevations are intended to represent the most significant points in terms of elevation gain and loss and provide the hiker with a general sense of the elevation change along each section of the hike. Of course, many ups and downs have not been referenced in this book, and the difficulty of the terrain may vary considerably. Hikers should use the elevations provided only as a general guide.

Also in the Features column are distances and compass direction to facilities located farther than 0.1 mile from the Trail. See more information about facilities below.

To the right of the list of features, **facilities,** if any, are noted with a one-letter code. In general, all facilities within five miles of the Trail by road are included, unless similar facilities are located closer to the footpath or a facility's inclusion would not significantly benefit the hiker. In some cases, where a specific facility is not available for a great distance, we have included facilities that are more than five miles from the Trail but still within 12 miles.

Shelters, campsites, and water sources are located within about 500 feet of the Trail unless a distance is listed in the Features column. Distances to all other facilities are always noted in the Features column.

## CODES

**C** *Campsites and campgrounds.* For New Hampshire, the "C" code is also used to indicate those shelters at which tent camping also is permitted.

**E** *"East,"* used to designate direction to facilities that are to the right of the Trail when traveling north (i.e., toward Katahdin).

**G** *Groceries, supplies.*

**L** *Lodgings other than Trail shelters, campsites, and campgrounds,* such as motels, hotels, cottages, and hostels. This code is also used for the Appalachian Mountain Club (AMC) huts in New Hampshire and camps (commercial cottages) in Maine.

**m** *Miles.*

**M** *Meals; restaurants.*

**nw** *No potable water.* This is used in shelter and campsite listings only.

**P.O.** *Post office.* Towns without post offices or that are far away from the Trail are listed only if the Trail goes directly through them; "P.O." is omitted in those cases.

**R** *Road access.* Only roads open to the public and passable by ordinary automobiles are designated. Included are road crossings and locations where the Trail runs along a road or is adjacent to a road that provides access to the Trail. Where the road crossings are frequent (every two miles or less), lesser ones are omitted.

**S** *Shelter.* A three-sided structure, with or without bunks or floors, intended as overnight housing for hikers (also known as lean-tos in some areas). Included in this category are unlocked cabins or lodges, found primarily in New Hampshire, Vermont, Pennsylvania, and Maryland. (See also "L".)

**W** *"West,"* used to designate direction to facilities that are to the left of the Trail when traveling north (i.e., toward Katahdin).

**w** *Water* (from springs, streams, etc.). In general, where available, water sources are listed about every three to four miles. Other water sources do exist, and not every water source is listed in the Data Book. **Note:** *All water should be purified before use.*

★ Indicates an **Appalachian Trail Community™,** a town designated by the ATC as a participant in A.T. protection work through local education initiatives and land conservation activity and known for being welcoming to A.T. hikers. A list of designated towns and counties can be found on page 95.

Whether you're planning to hike the A.T. for a day, a week, or for the entire length of the Trail, be prepared with current Trail information, appropriate equipment, and solid outdoor skills—and enjoy your hike!

# Appalachian Trail Distances

These sections and Trail points correspond to the beginning and endings of chapters in this book and the eleven-volume series of official Appalachian Trail guides, published by the Appalachian Trail Conservancy.

## LENGTH BY SECTION

| Section | Miles |
|---|---|
| Maine | 282.0 |
| New Hampshire–Vermont | 311.7 |
| Massachusetts–Connecticut | 142.4 |
| New York–New Jersey | 163.7 |
| Pennsylvania | 230.0 |
| Maryland–West Virginia–Northern Virginia | 95.2 |
| Shenandoah National Park | 107.8 |
| Central Virginia | 227.3 |
| Southwest Virginia | 166.8 |
| Tennessee–North Carolina | 304.0 |
| North Carolina–Georgia | 167.0 |

## CUMULATIVE DISTANCES

| | | |
|---|---|---|
| 0.0 | Baxter Peak, Katahdin, ME | 2,197.9 |
| 282.0 | Maine–New Hampshire line | 1,915.9 |
| 593.7 | Vermont–Massachusetts line | 1,604.2 |
| 736.1 | Connecticut–New York line | 1,461.8 |
| 899.8 | New Jersey–Pennsylvania line | 1,298.1 |
| 1,129.8 | Pennsylvania–Maryland line | 1,068.1 |
| 1,225.0 | Front Royal, VA | 972.9 |
| 1,332.8 | Rockfish Gap, VA | 865.1 |
| 1,560.1 | New River, VA | 637.8 |
| 1,726.9 | Damascus, VA | 471.0 |
| 2,030.9 | Fontana Dam, NC | 167.0 |
| 2,197.9 | Springer Mountain, GA | 0.0 |

# Maine

| Club | GBS | NtoS | Features | Facilities (see page 14 for codes) | StoN | Map |
|---|---|---|---|---|---|---|
| | | *Miles from Katahdin* | | | *Miles from ME–NH Line* | |
| Maine A.T. Club | Baxter State Park & 100-Mile Wilderness Section | 0.0 | Katahdin (*K'taadn*) (Baxter Peak) (5,268') | | 282.0 | Maine Map 1 |
| | | 1.0 | Abol Trail, Thoreau Spring | w | 281.0 | |
| | | 4.0 | Katahdin Stream Falls | w | 278.0 | |
| | | 5.2 | Katahdin Stream Campground, Birches Campsite (1,070') (C,S,w on A.T.) | CSw | 276.8 | |
| | | 5.3 | Cross Tote Road | R | 276.7 | |
| | | 7.5 | Daicey Pond Campground Road (L,w 0.1m E) | RLw | 274.5 | |
| | | 8.8 | Big Niagara Falls | w | 273.2 | |
| | | 9.6 | Upper Fork Nesowadnehunk Stream (ford) | w | 272.4 | |
| | | 10.5 | Lower Fork Nesowadnehunk Stream (ford) | w | 271.5 | |
| | | 11.0 | Pine Point | w | 271.0 | |
| | | 14.0 | Katahdin Stream | w | 268.0 | |
| | | 14.4 | Abol Stream, Baxter Park Boundary | | 267.6 | |
| | | 15.1 | Abol Bridge over West Branch of Penobscot River (C,G,w on A.T.) | RCGw | 266.9 | |
| | | 18.6 | Hurd Brook Lean-to (710') | Sw | 263.4 | |
| | | 21.1 | Rainbow Ledges (1,517') | | 260.9 | |
| | | 22.9 | Rainbow Lake (east end) | w | 259.1 | |
| | | 26.3 | Rainbow Spring Campsite | Cw | 255.7 | |
| | | 28.1 | Rainbow Lake (west end) Side Trail | w | 253.9 | |
| | | 30.1 | Rainbow Stream Lean-to (1,020') | Sw | 251.9 | |
| | | 32.5 | Pollywog Stream (682') | w | 249.5 | |
| | | 33.9 | Crescent Pond (west end) | w | 248.1 | |
| | | 36.3 | Nesuntabunt Mountain (1,520') | | 245.7 | |
| | | 38.2 | Wadleigh Stream Lean-to | Sw | 243.8 | |
| | | 40.8 | Nahmakanta Lake (south end) (650') | RCw | 241.2 | |
| | | 42.3 | Tumbledown Dick Trail | | 239.7 | |

# Maine

| Club | GBS | NtoS | Features | Facilities (see page 14 for codes) | StoN | Map |
|---|---|---|---|---|---|---|
| | | *Miles from Katahdin* | | | *Miles from ME–NH Line* | |
| Maine A.T. Club | Baxter State Park & 100-Mile Wilderness Section | 43.8 | Nahmakanta Stream Lean-to | Sw | 238.2 | Maine Map 2 |
| | | 45.7 | Mahar Tote Road (C 0.2m E) | C | 236.3 | |
| | | 47.7 | Pemadumcook Lake (southwest shore) | w | 234.3 | |
| | | 48.3 | Potaywadjo Spring Lean-to (710') | Sw | 233.7 | |
| | | 50.1 | Sand Beach, Lower Jo-Mary Lake | w | 231.9 | |
| | | 51.8 | Antlers Campsite (500') | Cw | 230.2 | |
| | | 53.1 | Mud Pond (outlet) | w | 228.9 | |
| | | 56.0 | Jo-Mary Road | Rw | 226.0 | |
| | | 59.7 | Cooper Brook Falls Lean-to (880') | Sw | 222.3 | |
| | | 62.0 | Crawford Pond (outlet) | w | 220.0 | |
| | | 62.9 | Johnston Pond Road | R | 219.1 | |
| | | 64.3 | Little Boardman Mountain (2,017') | | 217.7 | |
| | | 65.6 | Spring | w | 216.4 | |
| | | 65.9 | Mountain View Pond (outlet) | w | 216.1 | |
| | | 67.5 | East Branch of Pleasant River (ford) | w | 214.5 | |
| | | 67.8 | East Branch Lean-to (1,225') | Sw | 214.2 | |
| | | 69.4 | Logan Brook Road | w | 212.6 | |
| | | 71.4 | Logan Brook Lean-to (2,480') | Sw | 210.6 | |
| | | 72.8 | White Cap Mountain (3,650') | | 209.2 | |
| | | 73.9 | White Brook Trail | | 208.1 | |
| | | 74.5 | Hay Mountain (3,244') | | 207.5 | |
| | | 76.1 | West Peak | | 205.9 | |
| | | 76.8 | Sidney Tappan Campsite (2,425') | Cw | 205.2 | |
| | | 77.7 | Gulf Hagas Mountain (2,683') | | 204.3 | |
| | | 78.6 | Carl A. Newhall Lean-to (1,860') | Sw | 203.4 | |
| | | 82.1 | Gulf Hagas Cut-off Trail | w | 199.9 | |
| | | 82.8 | Gulf Hagas Rim Trail | w | 199.2 | |
| | | 83.8 | The Hermitage (695') (C,w 0.7m E) | Cw | 198.2 | |

# Maine

| Club | GBS | NtoS | Features | Facilities (see page 14 for codes) | StoN | Map |
|---|---|---|---|---|---|---|
| | | *Miles from Katahdin* | | | *Miles from ME–NH Line* | |
| Maine A.T. Club | | 84.1 | West Branch of Pleasant River (ford) | w | 197.9 | Maine Map 3 |
| | | 84.6 | Katahdin Iron Works Road | R | 197.4 | |
| | | 85.8 | East Chairback Pond Side Trail (1,630') (w 0.2m W) | w | 196.2 | |
| | | 88.0 | Chairback Mountain (2,219') | | 194.0 | |
| | | 88.5 | Chairback Gap Lean-to (1,930') | Sw | 193.5 | |
| | | 88.9 | Columbus Mountain (2,325') | | 193.1 | |
| | | 90.2 | West Chairback Pond Side Trail (1,770') | w | 191.8 | |
| | | 90.8 | Third Mountain, Monument Cliff (2,061') | | 191.2 | |
| | | 91.3 | Third Mountain Trail | | 190.7 | |
| | | 95.6 | Cloud Pond Lean-to Side Trail (S,w 0.3m E) | Sw | 186.4 | |
| | | 96.5 | Barren Mountain (2,670') | | 185.5 | |
| | | 99.6 | Long Pond Stream Lean-to (940') | Sw | 182.4 | |
| | | 100.4 | Long Pond Stream (ford) (620') | w | 181.6 | |
| | | 104.3 | Wilson Valley Lean-to (1,045') | Sw | 177.7 | |
| | | 104.7 | CPKC Railway | | 177.3 | |
| | | 105.0 | Big Wilson Stream (ford) (600') | w | 177.0 | |
| | | 107.9 | Little Wilson Falls Trail, Little Wilson Stream | w | 174.1 | |
| | | 108.1 | Little Wilson Falls | | 173.9 | |
| | | 110.7 | North Pond (outlet) | w | 171.3 | |
| | | 111.7 | Leeman Brook Lean-to (1,060') | Sw | 170.3 | |
| | | 112.8 | Lily Pond | w | 169.2 | |
| | | 113.5 | Bell Pond | w | 168.5 | |
| | | 114.6 | Spectacle Pond (outlet) | w | 167.4 | |
| | | 114.7 | ME-15 (1,215') | R | 167.3 | |
| | | 118.0 | **Monson, ME, P.O. 04464** (900') (P.O.,C,G,L,M 2m E) | ★ CGLM | 164.0 | |
| | | 121.0 | Shirley–Blanchard Road | R | 161.0 | Map 4 |
| | | 121.4 | East Branch of Piscataquis River (ford) | w | 160.6 | |

# Maine

| Club | GBS | NtoS | Features | Facilities (see page 14 for codes) | StoN | Map |
|---|---|---|---|---|---|---|
| | | *Miles from Katahdin* | | | *Miles from ME–NH Line* | |
| Maine A.T. Club | Kennebec Section | 123.7 | Horseshoe Canyon Lean-to (870') | Sw | 158.3 | Maine Map 4 |
| | | 126.8 | West Branch of Piscataquis River (ford) | w | 155.2 | |
| | | 130.5 | Bald Mountain Pond (outlet) (ford) | w | 151.5 | |
| | | 132.6 | Moxie Bald Lean-to (1,220') | Sw | 149.4 | |
| | | 134.7 | Moxie Bald Mountain (2,629') | | 147.3 | |
| | | 136.7 | Bald Mountain Brook Lean-to (1,300') | Sw | 145.3 | |
| | | 139.5 | Moxie Pond (south end) (970') | Rw | 142.5 | |
| | | 144.4 | Pleasant Pond Mountain (2,470') | | 137.6 | |
| | | 145.7 | Pleasant Pond Lean-to (1,320') | Sw | 136.3 | |
| | | 146.1 | Boise-Cascade Logging Road | R | 135.9 | |
| | | 148.7 | Holly Brook | w | 133.3 | |
| | | 151.4 | **US-201; Caratunk, ME, P.O. 04925** (P.O. 0.3m E; C,L,M 2.0m W) | RCLM | 130.6 | |
| | | 151.7 | Kennebec River (490') (ferry) | w | 130.3 | |
| | | 155.0 | Trail to Harrison's Pierce Pond Camps (L,M 0.3m E; w 0.1m E) | RLMw | 127.0 | Maine Map 5 |
| | | 155.4 | Pierce Pond Lean-to (1,160') | Sw | 126.6 | |
| | | 158.9 | North Branch of Carrying Place Stream | w | 123.1 | |
| | | 159.6 | Logging Road | R | 122.4 | |
| | | 161.3 | East Carry Pond (north end) | w | 120.7 | |
| | | 162.8 | Sandy Stream, Middle Carry Pond (inlet) | w | 119.2 | |
| | | 164.7 | West Carry Pond (east side) | w | 117.3 | |
| | | 165.4 | West Carry Pond Lean-to (1,340') | Sw | 116.6 | |
| | | 166.1 | West Carry Pond (west side) | w | 115.9 | |
| | | 167.2 | Roundtop Mountain (1,760') | | 114.8 | |
| | | 168.9 | Long Falls Dam Road (1,225') | R | 113.1 | |
| | | 170.5 | Flagstaff Lake | Cw | 111.5 | |
| | | 171.5 | Bog Brook Road, Flagstaff Lake (inlet) | Rw | 110.5 | |
| | | 171.6 | East Flagstaff Road | R | 110.4 | |
| | | 173.1 | Little Bigelow Lean-to (1,760') | Sw | 108.9 | |

# Maine

| Club | GBS | N to S Miles from Katahdin | Features | Facilities (see page 14 for codes) | S to N Miles from ME–NH Line | Map |
|---|---|---|---|---|---|---|
| Maine A.T. Club | High Peaks Section | 174.8 | Little Bigelow Mountain (east end) (3,010') | | 107.2 | Maine Map 5 |
| | | 178.0 | Safford Notch Campsite (2,230') (C,w 0.3m E) | Cw | 104.0 | |
| | | 178.1 | Safford Brook Trail | | 103.9 | |
| | | 180.0 | Bigelow Mountain (Avery Peak) (4,090') | | 102.0 | |
| | | 180.4 | Avery Memorial Campsite, Bigelow Col, Fire Warden's Trail | Cw | 101.6 | |
| | | 180.7 | Bigelow Mountain (West Peak) (4,145') | | 101.3 | |
| | | 182.8 | South Horn (3,805') | | 99.2 | |
| | | 183.3 | Horns Pond Lean-tos (3,160') | CSw | 98.7 | |
| | | 183.5 | Horns Pond Trail | | 98.5 | |
| | | 185.2 | Bigelow Range Trail, Cranberry Pond (w 0.2m W) | w | 96.8 | |
| | | 186.5 | Cranberry Stream Campsite (1,350') | Cw | 95.5 | |
| | | 187.4 | Stratton Brook (1,230') | w | 94.6 | |
| | | 187.6 | Stratton Brook Pond Road | R | 94.4 | |
| | | 188.4 | **ME-27; Stratton, ME, P.O. 04982** (P.O.,G,L,M 5m W; G,M 3m E) | RGLM | 93.6 | |
| | | 193.6 | North Crocker Mountain (4,228') | | 88.4 | Maine Map 6 |
| | | 194.6 | South Crocker Mountain (4,040') | | 87.4 | |
| | | 195.7 | Crocker Cirque Campsite Side Trail (2,710') (w on A.T.; C 0.2m E) | Cw | 86.3 | |
| | | 196.7 | Caribou Valley Road (2,220') | R | 85.3 | |
| | | 196.8 | South Branch Carrabassett River (ford) | w | 85.2 | |
| | | 199.0 | Sugarloaf Mountain Trail | | 83.0 | |
| | | 201.1 | Spaulding Mountain (4,000') | | 80.9 | |
| | | 201.9 | Spaulding Mountain Lean-to (3,140') | Sw | 80.1 | |
| | | 203.0 | Mt. Abraham Trail | | 79.0 | |
| | | 204.1 | Lone Mountain (3,280') | | 77.9 | |
| | | 207.2 | Orbeton Stream (ford) (1,550') | w | 74.8 | |

# Maine

| Club | GBS | NtoS | Features | Facilities (see page 14 for codes) | StoN | Map |
|---|---|---|---|---|---|---|
| | | *Miles from Katahdin* | | | *Miles from ME–NH Line* | |
| Maine A.T. Club | High Peaks Section | 209.9 | Poplar Ridge Lean-to (2,960') | Sw | 72.1 | Maine Map 6 |
| | | 211.3 | Saddleback Junior (3,655') | | 70.7 | |
| | | 212.6 | Redington Stream Campsite | Cw | 69.4 | |
| | | 213.3 | The Horn (4,040') | | 68.7 | |
| | | 214.3 | Berry Pickers Trail | | 67.7 | |
| | | 214.9 | Saddleback Mountain (4,120') | | 67.1 | |
| | | 216.9 | Eddy Pond | w | 65.1 | |
| | | 218.8 | Piazza Rock Lean-to (2,065') | Sw | 63.2 | |
| | | 220.5 | Sandy River (1,595') | w | 61.5 | |
| | | 220.6 | **ME-4; Rangeley, ME, P.O. 04970** (P.O.,C,G,L,M 9m W) | RCGLM | 61.4 | |
| | Western Maine Section | 222.7 | South Pond (2,174') | w | 59.3 | |
| | | 225.4 | Little Swift River Pond Campsite (2,460') | Cw | 56.6 | |
| | | 230.0 | Sabbath Day Pond Lean-to | Sw | 52.0 | |
| | | 230.3 | Long Pond (2,330') | w | 51.7 | |
| | | 232.1 | Moxie Pond | w | 49.9 | |
| | | 233.7 | **ME-17; Oquossoc, ME, P.O. 04964** (P.O.,G,L,M 11m W) | RGLM | 48.3 | |
| | | 234.5 | Bemis Stream (ford) (1,495') | w | 47.5 | Maine Map 7 |
| | | 238.3 | Bemis Mountain Lean-to (2,800') | Sw | 43.7 | |
| | | 240.0 | Bemis Range (West Peak) (3,592') | | 42.0 | |
| | | 240.8 | Bemis Stream Trail | | 41.2 | |
| | | 244.2 | Old Blue Mountain (3,600') | | 37.8 | |
| | | 247.0 | South Arm Road, Black Brook (ford) (1,410'), Black Brook Campsite (G 4.5m W) | RCGw | 35.0 | |
| | | 248.8 | Moody Mountain (2,440) | | 33.2 | |
| | | 249.7 | Sawyer Notch, Sawyer Brook (ford) (1,095') | w | 32.3 | |
| | | 251.1 | Hall Mountain Lean-to (2,650') | Sw | 30.9 | |
| | | 252.4 | Wyman Mountain (2,945') | | 29.6 | |
| | | 255.3 | Surplus Pond (outlet) | w | 26.7 | |

# Maine

| Club | GBS | N to S Miles from Katahdin | Features | Facilities (see page 14 for codes) | S to N Miles from ME–NH Line | Map |
|---|---|---|---|---|---|---|
| Maine A.T. Club | Western Maine Section | 257.1 | East B Hill Road (1,485'); **Andover, ME, P.O. 04216** (P.O.,C,G,M 8m E) | RCGM | 24.9 | Maine Map 7 |
| | | 257.9 | Dunn Notch and Falls | w | 24.1 | |
| | | 261.6 | Frye Notch Lean-to (2,280') | Sw | 20.4 | |
| | | 263.4 | Baldpate Mountain (East Peak), Grafton Loop Trail (3,810') | | 18.6 | |
| | | 264.3 | Baldpate Mountain (West Peak) (3,662') | | 17.7 | |
| | | 265.1 | Baldpate Lean-to (2,660') | Sw | 16.9 | |
| | | 267.4 | Grafton Notch, ME-26 (1,495') | R | 14.6 | |
| | | 268.5 | Brook | w | 13.5 | |
| Appalachian Mountain Club | | 270.9 | Old Speck Trail, Grafton Loop Trail (3,985') | | 11.1 | |
| | | 272.0 | Speck Pond Shelter and Campsite, Speck Pond Trail | CSw | 10.0 | |
| | | 272.9 | Mahoosuc Arm (3,770') | | 9.1 | |
| | | 274.4 | Mahoosuc Notch (east end) (2,150') | w | 7.6 | |
| | | 275.4 | Mahoosuc Notch (west end), Notch Trail | w | 6.6 | |
| | | 276.6 | Fulling Mill Mountain (South Peak) (3,395') | | 5.4 | |
| | | 276.9 | Full Goose Shelter and Campsite | CSw | 5.1 | |
| | | 277.9 | Goose Eye Mountain (North Peak) | | 4.1 | |
| | | 279.2 | Goose Eye Mountain (East Peak) (3,790') | | 2.8 | |
| | | 279.3 | Wright Trail | | 2.7 | |
| | | 279.6 | Goose Eye Trail | | 2.4 | |
| | | 281.0 | Mt. Carlo (3,565') | | 1.0 | |
| | | 281.4 | Carlo Col Trail, Carlo Col Shelter and Campsite (C,S,w 0.3m W) | CSw | 0.6 | |
| | | 282.0 | Maine–New Hampshire Line (2,972') | | 0.0 | |

# New Hampshire–Vermont

| Club | GBS | NtoS | Features | Facilities (see page 14 for codes) | StoN | Map |
|---|---|---|---|---|---|---|
| | | *Miles from ME-NH line* | | | *Miles from VT-MA line* | |
| Appalachian Mountain Club | NH Section 1 | 0.0 | Maine–New Hampshire Line (2,972') | | 311.7 | NH-VT Map 1 |
| | | 1.9 | Mt. Success (3,565') | | 309.8 | |
| | | 4.7 | Gentian Pond Shelter/Campsite (2,166') | CSw | 307.0 | |
| | | 5.4 | Moss Pond | w | 306.3 | |
| | | 6.9 | Dream Lake | w | 304.8 | |
| | | 9.6 | Trident Col Tentsite (2,020') | Cw | 302.1 | |
| | | 10.7 | Cascade Mountain (2,631') | | 301.0 | |
| | | 15.0 | Brook | w | 296.7 | |
| | | 16.2 | Androscoggin River (750') | R | 295.5 | |
| | NH Section 2 | 16.5 | US-2; **Gorham, NH, P.O. 03581** | ★ | | |
| | | | (w on A.T.; P.O.,G,L,M 3.6m W; C,L,M 1.8m W) | RCGLMw | 295.2 | NH-VT Map 2 |
| | | 18.4 | Rattle River Shelter | Sw | 293.3 | |
| | | 22.4 | Mt. Moriah (4,049') | | 289.3 | |
| | | 24.5 | Imp Shelter/Campsite (3,250') | CSw | 287.2 | |
| | | 27.0 | Middle Carter Mountain (4,610') | | 284.7 | |
| | | 29.1 | Zeta Pass (3,890') | | 282.6 | |
| | | 30.5 | Carter Dome (4,832') | | 281.2 | |
| | | 31.0 | Spring | w | 280.7 | |
| | | 31.7 | Carter Notch, Carter Notch Hut* (3,350') (L,M,w 0.2m E) | LMw | 280.0 | |

The footbridge over the West Branch of the Peabody River (mile 41.6) has been closed by the U.S. Forest Service due to structural failure. A temporary 6.4-mile detour between Carter Notch (mile 31.7) and Osgood Tentsite (mile 42.4), using the Nineteen Mile Brook, Great Gulf, and Osgood Trails, has been marked with white blazes. It is possible to ford the river but only in very dry conditions. Using the detour is recommended. For more information, go to appalachiantrail.org/MadisonGulfBridge.

| NtoS | Features | Facilities | StoN |
|---|---|---|---|
| 32.6 | Wildcat Mountain, Peak A (4,422') | | 279.1 |
| 34.6 | Wildcat Mountain, Peak D | | 277.1 |

# New Hampshire–Vermont

| Club | GBS | NtoS | Features | Facilities (see page 14 for codes) | StoN | Map |
|---|---|---|---|---|---|---|
| | | *Miles from ME-NH line* | | | *Miles from VT-MA line* | |
| Randolph Mountain Club | NH Section 3 | 37.6 | Pinkham Notch, NH 16, Pinkham Notch Camp (2,050') (L,M,w on A.T.) | RLMw | 274.1 | NH-VT Map 2 |
| | | 39.7 | Lowe's Bald Spot (2,860') | | 272.0 | |
| | | 41.6 | West Branch, Peabody River (2,300') | w | 270.1 | |
| | | 42.4 | Osgood Tentsite | Cw | 269.3 | |
| | | 44.9 | Mt. Madison (5,366') | | 266.8 | |
| | | 45.4 | Madison Spring Hut, Valley Way Tentsite (C,w 0.6m W; L,M,w on A.T.) | CLMw | 266.3 | |
| | | 46.3 | Thunderstorm Junction, Spur Trail to Crag Camp Cabin, Lowe's Path to Mt. Adams & Gray Knob Cabin (S,w 1.1m W, 1.2m W) | Sw | 265.4 | |
| | | 46.9 | Israel Ridge Path to The Perch Shelter (C,S,w 0.9m W) | CSw | 264.8 | |
| Appalachian Mountain Club | | 47.6 | Edmands Col (4,938') | | 264.1 | |
| | | 51.1 | **Mt. Washington, NH, P.O. 03589** (6,288') (P.O.,M on A.T.) | RM | 260.6 | |
| | | 52.5 | Lakes of the Clouds Hut (5,012') (L,M,w on A.T.) | LMw | 259.2 | |
| | | 53.6 | Mt. Franklin | | 258.1 | |
| | | 54.2 | Spring | w | 257.5 | |
| | | 55.5 | Spring | w | 256.2 | |
| | | 56.4 | Mt. Pierce (Mt. Clinton) | | 255.3 | |
| | | 57.2 | Mizpah Spring Hut, Nauman Tentsite (3,800') (C,L,M,w on A.T.) | CLMw | 254.5 | |
| | | 58.9 | Mt. Jackson | | 252.8 | |

# New Hampshire–Vermont

| Club | GBS | NtoS | Features | Facilities (see page 14 for codes) | StoN | Map |
|---|---|---|---|---|---|---|
| | | *Miles from ME-NH line* | | | *Miles from VT-MA line* | |
| Appalachian Mountain Club | NH Section 4 | 60.3 | Mt. Webster (3,910') | | 251.4 | NH-VT Map 2 |
| | | 63.5 | Saco River | | 248.2 | |
| | | 63.6 | Crawford Notch, US-302, Dry River Campground (1,275') (C 1.8m E; M 1m W; C,G,L 3m E; L,M 3.7m W) | RCGLM | 248.1 | |
| | | 66.5 | Ethan Pond Shelter/Campsite (2,860') | CSw | 245.2 | NH-VT Map 3 |
| | | 71.3 | Zealand Falls Hut (2,630') (L,M,w on A.T.) | LMw | 240.4 | |
| | | 72.5 | Zeacliff | | 239.2 | |
| | | 75.5 | Mt. Guyot, Guyot Shelter/Campsite (4,580') (C,S,w 0.8m E) | CSw | 236.2 | |
| | | 77.5 | South Twin Mountain, North Twin Spur (4,902') | | 234.2 | |
| | | 78.3 | Galehead Hut (L,M,w on A.T.) | LMw | 233.4 | |
| | | 81.0 | Garfield Ridge Shelter/Campsite (3,900') | CSw | 230.7 | |
| | | 81.4 | Mt. Garfield (4,500') | | 230.3 | |
| | | 84.9 | Mt. Lafayette, Greenleaf Hut (5,260') (L,M 1.1m W; w 0.2m W) | LMw | 226.8 | |
| | | 85.9 | Mt. Lincoln | | 225.8 | |
| | | 86.6 | Little Haystack Mountain | | 225.1 | |
| | | 88.7 | Liberty Spring Tentsite (3,870') | Cw | 223.0 | |
| | NH Section 5 | 91.3 | Franconia Notch, US-3, Lafayette Place Campground (1,450'); **North Woodstock, NH, P.O. 03262** (P.O.,G,L,M 5.8m E; G,L,M 2.2m E; C 2.5m W; L 1.6m E) | RCGLM | 220.4 | |
| | | 94.2 | Lonesome Lake Hut (2,760') (L,M,w on A.T.) | LMw | 217.5 | |

# New Hampshire–Vermont

| Club | GBS | NtoS<br>*Miles from ME-NH line* | Features | Facilities (see page 14 for codes) | StoN<br>*Miles from VT-MA line* | Map |
|---|---|---|---|---|---|---|
| *AMC* | NH Section 5 | 96.1 | Kinsman Pond Shelter/Campsite | CSw | 215.6 | |
| | | 96.7 | North Kinsman Mountain | | 215.0 | |
| | | 97.6 | South Kinsman Mountain (4,358') | | 214.1 | |
| | | 100.1 | Eliza Brook Shelter/Campsite (2,400') | CSw | 211.6 | |
| | | 103.0 | Mt. Wolf (East Peak) (3,478') | | 208.7 | |
| *Dartmouth Outing Club* | NH Section 6 | 107.6 | Kinsman Notch, NH 112 (1,870') | R | 204.1 | NH-VT Map 4 |
| | | 109.1 | Beaver Brook Shelter (3,750') | Sw | 202.6 | |
| | | 111.4 | Mt. Moosilauke (4,802') | | 200.3 | |
| | | 116.0 | Jeffers Brook Shelter (1,350') | Sw | 195.7 | |
| | NH Section 7 | 117.1 | NH-25 (1,000'); **Glencliff, NH, P.O. 03238** (P.O.,L 0.5m E) | RL | 194.6 | |
| | | 119.5 | Mt. Mist (2,200') | | 192.2 | |
| | | 122.0 | NH-25C (1,550'); **Warren, NH, P.O. 03279** (w on A.T.; P.O.,G,M 4m E) | RGMw | 189.7 | |
| | | 124.6 | Ore Hill | Cw | 187.1 | |
| | | 125.2 | Cape Moonshine Road | R | 186.5 | |
| | NH Section 8 | 126.8 | NH-25A (900'); **Wentworth, NH, P.O. 03282** (P.O.,G,L 4.3m E) | RG | 184.9 | |
| | | 130.1 | Side trail to Mt. Cube (North Summit) (2,911') | | 181.6 | |
| | | 131.7 | Hexacuba Shelter (w on A.T.; S 0.3m E) | Sw | 180.0 | |
| | | 133.1 | South Jacob's Brook (1,450') | w | 178.6 | |
| | | 137.0 | Firewarden's Cabin (3,230') | Sw | 174.7 | |
| | | 137.1 | Smarts Mountain Tentsite | Cw | 174.6 | |
| | | 140.8 | Lyme–Dorchester Road | Rw | 170.9 | |
| | | 142.8 | Dartmouth Skiway (880'); | | | |

# New Hampshire–Vermont

| Club | GBS | NtoS | Features | Facilities (see page 14 for codes) | StoN | Map |
|---|---|---|---|---|---|---|
| | | *Miles from ME-NH line* | | | *Miles from VT-MA line* | |
| Dartmouth Outing Club | NH Section 9 | | **Lyme, NH, P.O. 03768** (P.O.,G,L,M 3.2m W) | RGLM | 168.9 | NH-VT Map 5 |
| | | 143.7 | Trapper John Shelter (S,w 0.2m W) | Sw | 168.0 | |
| | | 144.2 | Holts Ledge (1,930') | | 167.5 | |
| | | 146.2 | Goose Pond Road (952') | R | 165.5 | |
| | | 147.5 | South Fork Hewes Brook | w | 164.2 | |
| | | 149.4 | Moose Mountain Shelter | Sw | 162.3 | |
| | | 150.2 | Moose Mountain (South Peak) (2,290') | | 161.5 | |
| | | 151.8 | Mink Brook | w | 159.9 | |
| | | 152.0 | Three Mile Road | R | 159.7 | |
| | | 154.5 | Etna–Hanover Center Road (845'); **Etna, NH, P.O. 03750** (P.O. 1.2m E) | R | 157.2 | |
| | | 155.9 | Trescott Road | R | 155.8 | |
| | | 158.4 | Ledyard Spring (w 0.2m W) | w | 153.3 | |
| | | 158.9 | Velvet Rocks Shelter (S 0.2m W) | S | 152.8 | |
| | | 159.7 | NH-120 | R | 152.0 | |
| | | 160.4 | Dartmouth College; **Hanover, NH, P.O. 03755** (P.O.,G,L,M on A.T.) | ★ RGLM | 151.3 | |
| Green Mountain Club | VT Section 1 | 160.9 | New Hampshire–Vermont Line, Connecticut River (400') | R | 150.8 | |
| | | 161.9 | **Norwich, VT, P.O. 05055** (P.O.,G,L,M 0.3m W) | ★ RGLM | 149.8 | |
| | | 166.2 | Happy Hill Shelter/Campsite (1,460') | CSw | 145.5 | |
| | | 168.8 | Podunk Brook, Podunk Road | Rw | 142.9 | |
| | | 169.6 | Tigertown Road, Podunk Road | R | 142.1 | |

# New Hampshire–Vermont

| Club | GBS | NtoS Miles from ME-NH line | Features | Facilities (see page 14 for codes) | StoN Miles from VT-MA line | Map |
|---|---|---|---|---|---|---|
| Green Mountain Club | VT Section 2 | 170.2 | VT-14, White River (400'); **Hartford, VT, P.O. 05047** (P.O. 8m E) | Rw | 141.5 | NH-VT Map 5 |
| | | 173.5 | Joe Ranger Road | R | 138.2 | |
| | | 175.0 | Thistle Hill Shelter | Sw | 136.7 | |
| | | 175.3 | Thistle Hill (1,800') | | 136.4 | |
| | | 177.3 | Cloudland Road | R | 134.4 | |
| | | 179.1 | Pomfret–South Pomfret Road | Rw | 132.6 | |
| | | 181.3 | Woodstock Stage Road (820'); **South Pomfret, VT, P.O. 05067** (w on A.T.; P.O.,G 0.9m E) | RGw | 130.4 | |
| | VT Section 3 | 183.5 | VT-12 (882'); **Woodstock, VT, P.O. 05091** (P.O.,G,L,M 4.4m E) | RGLM | 128.2 | |
| | | 187.3 | Wintturi Shelter (1,900') (S,w 0.2m W) | Sw | 124.4 | NH-VT Map 6 |
| | | 189.7 | Side trail to The Lookout | | 122.0 | |
| | | 192.5 | Chateauguay Road | R | 119.2 | |
| | | 197.2 | Stony Brook Shelter (1,760') | Sw | 114.5 | |
| | | 201.5 | River Road (1,214') | R | 110.2 | |
| | | 202.0 | Thundering Brook Road | R | 109.7 | |
| | | 203.2 | Kent Pond (L,M,w on A.T.) | RLMw | 108.5 | |
| | | 203.9 | VT-100, Gifford Woods State Park | RCSw | 107.8 | |
| | | 205.3 | Sherburne Pass Trail (2,440') | | 106.4 | |
| | | 206.2 | Maine Junction; Junction with Long Trail; Tucker-Johnson Shelter (S 0.2m W) | S | 105.5 | |
| | | 207.2 | US-4 (1,880'); **Killington, VT, P.O. 05751** (P.O.,G 2.2m E; L,M 0.9m E) | RGLM | 104.5 | |

# New Hampshire–Vermont

| Club | GBS | NtoS Miles from ME-NH line | Features | Facilities (see page 14 for codes) | StoN Miles from VT-MA line | Map |
|---|---|---|---|---|---|---|
| Green Mountain Club | VT Section 4 | 209.1 | Churchill Scott Shelter | CSw | 102.6 | NH-VT Map 6 |
| | | 211.0 | Sherburne Pass Trail, Pico Camp (3,480') (S,w 0.5m E) | Sw | 100.7 | |
| | | 213.5 | Cooper Lodge, Killington Peak Trail (3,900') (C,S,w on A.T.; M 0.2m E) | CMSw | 98.2 | |
| | | 217.8 | Governor Clement Shelter (1,850') | Sw | 93.9 | |
| | | 219.4 | Upper Cold River Road | Rw | 92.3 | |
| | | 220.2 | Gould Brook (1,480') | w | 91.5 | |
| | | 221.0 | Cold River Road (Lower Road) | R | 90.7 | |
| | | 223.0 | Lottery Road | R | 88.7 | |
| | | 223.4 | Beacon Hill | | 88.3 | |
| | | 223.9 | Clarendon Shelter | CSw | 87.8 | |
| | | 224.9 | VT-103 (860'); **North Clarendon, VT, P.O. 05759** (P.O. 4.2m W; G 0.8m W) | RG | 86.8 | |
| | VT Section 5 | 225.0 | Clarendon Gorge, Mill River Suspension Bridge | w | 86.7 | |
| | | 227.6 | Minerva Hinchey Shelter (1,530') | CSw | 84.1 | |
| | | 231.2 | VT-140 (1,160'); **Wallingford, VT, P.O. 05773** (w on A.T.; P.O.,G,L,M 2.7m W; G 3.7m E) | RGLMw | 80.5 | |
| | | 231.3 | Sugar Hill Road | R | 80.4 | NH-VT Map 7 |
| | | 232.7 | Greenwall Shelter (S,w 0.2m E) | Sw | 79.0 | |
| | | 233.2 | Trail to White Rocks Cliff (2,400') | | 78.5 | |
| | | 237.2 | Green Mountain Trail to Homer Stone Brook Trail | | 74.5 | |

# New Hampshire–Vermont

| Club | GBS | NtoS<br>Miles from ME-NH line | Features | Facilities (see page 14 for codes) | StoN<br>Miles from VT-MA line | Map |
|---|---|---|---|---|---|---|
| Green Mountain Club | VT Section 6 | 237.4 | Spring | w | 74.3 | NH-VT Map 7 |
| | | 237.5 | Little Rock Pond Shelter and Tenting Area | CSw | 74.2 | |
| | | 239.5 | Danby–Landgrove Road (USFS-10), Black Branch (1,500'); **Danby, VT, P.O. 05739** (P.O.,G,M 3.2m W) | RGM | 72.2 | |
| | | 240.8 | Big Branch Shelter | CSw | 70.9 | |
| | | 241.0 | Old Job Trail to Old Job Shelter (C,S,w 1.3m E) | CSw | 70.7 | |
| | | 242.5 | Lost Pond Shelter | CSw | 69.2 | |
| | | 244.5 | Baker Peak (2,850') | | 67.2 | |
| | | 246.5 | Griffith Lake (north end) | w | 65.2 | |
| | | 246.7 | Griffith Lake Tenting Area | Cw | 65.0 | |
| | | 247.2 | Peru Peak Shelter | CSw | 64.5 | |
| | | 248.5 | Peru Peak (3,429') | | 63.2 | |
| | | 250.2 | Styles Peak | | 61.5 | |
| | | 251.8 | Mad Tom Notch, USFS-21 (2,446'); **Peru, VT, P.O. 05152** (P.O.,G 4m E; C 2.5m E) | RCGw | 59.9 | |
| | | 254.3 | Bromley Mountain (3,260') | | 57.4 | |
| | | 255.3 | Bromley Shelter | CSw | 56.4 | |
| | VT Section 7 | 257.3 | VT-11 & VT-30 (1,840'); **Manchester Center, VT, P.O. 05255** (P.O.,G,L,M 5.8m W; G 2.5m E; L,M 2.1m E) | ★ RGLM | 54.4 | |
| | | 259.7 | Spruce Peak | | 52.0 | |
| | | 260.1 | Spruce Peak Shelter | CSw | 51.6 | |
| | | 262.2 | Old Rootville Road, Prospect Rock | R | 49.5 | |
| | | 263.1 | Branch Pond Trail to William B. Douglas Shelter | | | |

# New Hampshire–Vermont

| Club | GBS | NtoS Miles from ME-NH line | Features | Facilities (see page 14 for codes) | StoN Miles from VT-MA line | Map |
|---|---|---|---|---|---|---|
| Green Mountain Club | VT Section 7 | | (S,w 0.5m W) | Sw | 48.6 | NH-VT Map 7 |
| | | 265.9 | Winhall River | w | 45.8 | |
| | | 267.8 | Lye Brook Trail to Stratton Pond Campsites and Shelter (2,555') (w on A.T.; C,w 0.7m W) | CSw | 43.9 | |
| | | 268.0 | Stratton Pond Trail | w | 43.7 | |
| | | 271.0 | Stratton Mountain (3,936') (G,M 1.7m E) | GM | 40.7 | |
| | VT Section 8 | 274.8 | Stratton–Arlington Road (Kelley Stand Road) (2,230') | Rw | 36.9 | NH-VT Map 8 |
| | | 278.4 | Story Spring Shelter | CSw | 33.3 | |
| | | 279.3 | South Alder Brook | w | 32.4 | |
| | | 283.0 | Kid Gore Shelter, Caughnawaga Tentsites | CSw | 28.7 | |
| | | 287.0 | Glastenbury Mountain (3,748') | | 24.7 | |
| | | 287.3 | Goddard Shelter | Sw | 24.4 | |
| | | 289.8 | Glastenbury Lookout (2,920') | | 21.9 | |
| | | 291.6 | Little Pond Lookout (3,060') | | 20.1 | |
| | | 294.2 | Hell Hollow Brook | w | 17.5 | |
| | | 295.8 | Melville Nauheim Shelter | Sw | 15.9 | |
| | VT Section 9 | 297.4 | City Stream, VT-9 (1,360'); **Bennington, VT, P.O. 05201** (P.O.,G,L,M 5m W; L 2.7m E; G 3.9m W) | ★ RGLMw | 14.3 | |
| | | 299.2 | Harmon Hill (2,325') | | 12.5 | |
| | | 301.7 | Congdon Shelter | CSw | 10.0 | |
| | | 305.9 | Roaring Branch | w | 5.8 | |
| | | 306.5 | Seth Warner Shelter | CSw | 5.2 | |
| | | 308.6 | County Road | R | 3.1 | |
| | | 311.3 | Brook | w | 0.4 | |
| | | 311.7 | Vermont–Massachusetts Line, southern end of Long Trail (2,330') | | 0.0 | |

# Massachusetts–Connecticut

| Club | GBS | NtoS | Features | Facilities (see page 14 for codes) | StoN | Map |
|---|---|---|---|---|---|---|
| | | *Miles from VT-MA line* | | | *Miles from CT-NY line* | |
| AMC Western Massachusetts Chapter | MA Section 1 | 0.0 | Vermont–Massachusetts Line, southern end of Long Trail (2,330') | | 142.4 | MA-CT Map 1 |
| | | 1.3 | Pine Cobble Trail | | 141.1 | |
| | | 2.3 | Sherman Brook Primitive Campsite | Cw | 140.1 | |
| | MA Section 2 | 4.1 | MA-2 (650'); **North Adams, MA, P.O. 01247; Williamstown, MA, P.O. 01267** (P.O.,G,L,M 2.5m E, 2.9m W; G 2.4m E; M 0.7m E; G,M 0.5m W; L 1.6m W) | ★ RGLM | 138.3 | |
| | | 5.0 | Pattison Road | Rw | 137.4 | |
| | | 7.1 | Wilbur Clearing Shelter (2,300') (C,S,w 0.3m W) | CSw | 135.3 | |
| | | 7.2 | Notch Road | R | 135.2 | |
| | | 10.4 | Mt. Greylock, Summit Road, Bascom Lodge (3,491') (L,M,w on A.T.) | RLMw | 132.0 | |
| | | 10.9 | Notch Road, Rockwell Road | R | 131.5 | |
| | | 13.1 | Jones Nose Trail | | 129.3 | |
| | | 13.7 | Mark Noepel Shelter (2,800') (C,S,w 0.2m E) | CSw | 128.7 | |
| | | 14.6 | Old Adams Road | | 127.8 | |
| | | 17.3 | Outlook Avenue | R | 125.1 | |
| | MA Section 3 | 18.1 | MA-8 (1,000'); **Cheshire, MA, P.O. 01225** (G 0.2m W, L 0.8m E) | ★ RGL | 124.3 | |
| | | 18.6 | Church Street, School Street (P.O.,C,M, w on A.T) | CRMw | 123.8 | |
| | | 19.8 | Cheshire Cobbles | | 122.6 | |
| | | 22.3 | Gore Pond (2,050') | | 120.1 | |

# Massachusetts–Connecticut

| Club | GBS | NtoS | Features | Facilities (see page 14 for codes) | StoN | Map |
|---|---|---|---|---|---|---|
| | | *Miles from VT-MA line* | | | *Miles from CT-NY line* | |
| AMC Western Massachusetts Chapter | MA Sec. 3 | 22.7 | Crystal Mountain Campsite (C,w 0.2m E) | Cw | 119.7 | MA-CT Map 1 |
| | | 26.4 | Gulf Road | R | 116.0 | |
| | MA Section 4 | 27.4 | MA-8, MA-9 (1,200'); **Dalton, MA, P.O. 01226** (M on A.T.; P.O.,G,L,M 0.3m W) | RL | 115.0 | |
| | | 28.0 | CSX Railroad | | 114.4 | |
| | | 30.1 | Grange Hall Road | R | 112.3 | |
| | | 30.4 | Kay Wood Shelter (C,S,w 0.2m E) | CSw | 112.0 | MA-CT Map 2 |
| | | 33.1 | Warner Hill (2,050') | | 109.3 | |
| | | 33.8 | Blotz Road | R | 108.6 | |
| | | 35.0 | Cady Brook | w | 107.4 | |
| | MA Section 5 | 37.0 | Pittsfield Road (Washington Mountain Road); (G,L 4.6m E; M 1.8m E) | RGLM | 105.4 | |
| | | 38.5 | West Branch Road | R | 103.9 | |
| | | 39.2 | October Mountain Shelter (1,950') | CSw | 103.2 | |
| | | 41.0 | County Road | R | 101.4 | |
| | | 43.3 | Finerty Pond | w | 99.1 | |
| | | 45.1 | Becket Mountain (2,180') | | 97.3 | |
| | | 45.6 | Tyne Road | R | 96.8 | |
| | MA Section 6 | 46.4 | U.S. 20 (1,400'); **Lee, MA, P.O. 01238** (P.O.,G,L,M 5m W) (L 0.2m E) | RGLM | 96.0 | |
| | | 46.7 | Greenwater Brook | w | 95.7 | |
| | | 46.8 | Massachusetts Turnpike | | 95.6 | |
| | | 48.0 | Upper Goose Pond Cabin (C,S,w 0.5m W) | CSw | 94.4 | |
| | | 48.8 | Upper Goose Pond | | 93.6 | |
| | | 50.7 | Goose Pond Road | R | 91.7 | |

# Massachusetts–Connecticut

Club: AMC Western Massachusetts Chapter
GBS: MA Section 7; MA Section 8
Map: MA-CT Map 2

| NtoS<br>*Miles from VT-MA line* | Features | Facilities<br>(see page 14 for codes) | StoN<br>*Miles from CT-NY line* |
|---|---|---|---|
| 52.7 | Brook | w | 89.7 |
| 53.1 | Webster Road (1,800') | R | 89.3 |
| 55.0 | Tyringham Main Road (930') | R | 87.4 |
| 56.1 | Jerusalem Road | RLw | 86.3 |
| | **Tyringham, MA, P.O. 01264** | | |
| | (P.O., L 0.6m W) | | |
| 58.1 | Shaker Campsite | Cw | 84.3 |
| 58.4 | Jerusalem Road (Fernside Road) | | |
| | (w 0.2m E) | Rw | 84.0 |
| 61.6 | Beartown Mountain Road | Rw | 80.8 |
| 62.2 | Mt. Wilcox North Shelter (2,100') | | |
| | (C,S,w 0.3m E) | CSw | 80.2 |
| 63.9 | Mt. Wilcox South Shelter | CSw | 78.5 |
| 64.7 | The Ledges | | 77.7 |
| 65.3 | Benedict Pond | | |
| | (C,w 0.5m w) | RCw | 77.1 |
| 66.1 | Blue Hill Road (Stony Brook Road) | R | 76.3 |
| 67.3 | MA- 23 (1,000'); | | |
| | **Great Barrington, MA, P.O. 01230** | ★ | |
| | (P.O.,G,L,M 4m W) | RGLM | 75.1 |
| 68.2 | Lake Buel Road | | |
| | (L,M 2.5m W) | RLM | 74.2 |
| 69.3 | Ice Gulch, Tom Leonard Shelter | | |
| | (C,S on A.T.; w 0.2m E) | CSw | 73.1 |
| 71.4 | East Mountain (1,800') | w | 71.0 |
| 72.8 | Home Road | R | 69.6 |
| 74.8 | Housatonic River | R | 67.6 |
| 75.7 | U.S. 7; Sheffield, MA., P.O. 01257 | | |
| | (P.O.,G,L,M 3.3m E; M 1.0m W, 0.8m E) | RGLM | 66.7 |
| 77.5 | Sheffield–Egremont Road (700') | R | 64.9 |

# Massachusetts–Connecticut

| Club | GBS | NtoS | Features | Facilities (see page 14 for codes) | StoN | Map |
|---|---|---|---|---|---|---|
| | | *Miles from VT-MA line* | | | *Miles from CT-NY line* | |
| AMC Western Massachusetts Chapter | MA Sec. 9 | 79.3 | MA-41 (Undermountain Road); **South Egremont, MA, P.O. 01258** (P.O.,G,M 1.2m W) | RGM | 63.1 | MA-CT Map 3 |
| | MA Section 10 | 80.2 | Jug End Road (Curtiss Road) (w 0.3m E) | Rw | 62.2 | |
| | | 81.3 | Jug End (1,750') | | 61.1 | |
| | | 83.0 | Elbow Trail | | 59.4 | |
| | | 83.6 | Glen Brook Shelter | CSw | 58.8 | |
| | | 83.7 | The Hemlocks Shelter | Sw | 58.7 | |
| | | 84.1 | Guilder Pond Picnic Area | R | 58.3 | |
| | | 84.8 | Mt. Everett (2,602') | | 57.6 | |
| | | 85.5 | Race Brook Falls Trail to Race Brook Campsite (C,w 0.4m E) | Cw | 56.9 | |
| | | 86.4 | Mt. Race | | 56.0 | |
| | | 88.2 | Side trail to Laurel Ridge Campsite | Cw | 54.2 | |
| AMC Connecticut Chapter | CT Section 1 | 89.2 | Sages Ravine (1,340') | w | 53.2 | |
| | | 89.8 | Sages Ravine Campsite | Cw | 52.6 | |
| | | 90.2 | Massachusetts–Connecticut Line | | 52.2 | |
| | | 90.7 | Bear Mountain (2,316') | | 51.7 | |
| | | 91.3 | Bear Mountain Road | | 51.1 | |
| | | 91.5 | Riga Junction, Undermountain Trail | | 50.9 | |
| | | 92.0 | Brassie Brook (South Branch), Brassie Brook Shelter | CSw | 50.4 | |
| | | 92.6 | Ball Brook Group Campsite | Cw | 49.8 | |
| | | 93.2 | Riga Shelter | CSw | 49.2 | |
| | | 94.0 | Lions Head (1,738') | | 48.4 | |
| | CT Section 2 | 96.2 | CT-41 (Under Mountain Road); **Salisbury, CT, P.O. 06068** (P.O.,G,L,M 0.8m W) | RGLM | 46.2 | |
| | | 96.9 | US-44 (700') | R | 45.5 | |
| | | 99.7 | Billy's View | | 42.7 | |

# Massachusetts–Connecticut

| Club | GBS | NtoS | Features | Facilities (see page 14 for codes) | StoN | Map |
|---|---|---|---|---|---|---|
| | | *Miles from VT-MA line* | | | *Miles from CT-NY line* | |
| AMC Connecticut Chapter | CT Section 2 | 100.5 | Rand's View | | 41.9 | MA-CT Map 3 |
| | | 100.6 | Side trail to Limestone Spring Shelter (C,S,w 0.5m W) | CSw | 41.8 | |
| | | 101.3 | Prospect Mountain (1,475') | | 41.1 | |
| | | 103.5 | Spring | w | 38.9 | |
| | | 104.6 | Housatonic River Road | R | 37.8 | |
| | | 105.0 | Housatonic River; **Falls Village, CT, P.O. 06031** (P.O. 0.5m E) | R | 37.4 | |
| | | 106.8 | Mohawk Trail (L,M 0.2m E) | LM | 35.6 | |
| | | 106.9 | US-7, Housatonic River (500') | R | 35.5 | |
| | | 107.5 | US-7, CT-112 | R | 34.9 | |
| | CT Section 3 | 107.9 | Belter's Campsite | Cw | 34.5 | |
| | | 110.1 | Hang Glider View | | 32.3 | |
| | | 110.9 | Sharon Mountain Campsite | Cw | 31.5 | |
| | | 112.1 | **Mt. Easter (1,350')** | | 30.3 | |
| | | 112.4 | Mt. Easter Road | R | 30.0 | |
| | | 113.3 | Pine Swamp Brook Shelter | CSw | 29.1 | |
| | | 114.4 | West Cornwall Road (800'); **West Cornwall, CT, P.O. 06796** (P.O. 2.2m E) | R | 28.0 | |
| | | 114.5 | Carse Brook | w | 27.9 | |
| | | 116.7 | Cesar Brook Campsite | Cw | 25.7 | |
| | | 117.8 | Pine Knob Loop Trail | | 24.6 | |
| | | 117.9 | Hatch Brook | w | 24.5 | |
| | | 119.0 | Old Sharon Road | R | 23.4 | |
| | | 119.1 | Guinea Brook | w | 23.3 | |
| | | 119.2 | CT-4; **Cornwall Bridge, CT, P.O. 06754** (P.O.,G,L 0.9m E) | RGL | 23.2 | |

# Massachusetts–Connecticut

| Club | GBS | NtoS<br>Miles from VT-MA line | Features | Facilities (see page 14 for codes) | StoN<br>Miles from CT-NY line | Map |
|---|---|---|---|---|---|---|
| AMC Connecticut Chapter | CT Section 4 | 120.1 | Silver Hill Campsite (1,000') | C(nw) | 22.3 | MA-CT Map 4 |
| | | 120.9 | River Road, Spring | Rw | 21.5 | |
| | | 122.9 | Stony Brook Campsite | Cw | 19.5 | |
| | | 123.3 | Stewart Hollow Brook Shelter (400') | CSw | 19.1 | |
| | | 125.6 | River Road | R | 16.8 | |
| | | 126.1 | St. Johns Ledges | | 16.3 | |
| | | 126.8 | Caleb's Peak (1,160') | | 15.6 | |
| | | 127.5 | Skiff Mountain Road | R | 14.9 | |
| | CT Section 5 (NY Section 1) | 130.5 | **CT-341, Schaghticoke Road (350'); Kent, CT, P.O. 06757** (P.O.,G,L,M 0.8m E) | RGLM | 11.9 | |
| | | 130.8 | Mt. Algo Shelter | CSw | 11.6 | |
| | | 131.8 | Thayer Brook | w | 10.6 | |
| | | 133.7 | Schaghticoke Mountain Campsite | Cw | 8.7 | |
| | | 135.1 | Connecticut–New York Line (1,250') | | 7.3 | |
| | | 136.3 | **Schaghticoke Mountain** | | 6.1 | |
| | | 137.0 | Connecticut–New York Line (1,000') | | 5.4 | |
| | | 138.0 | Schaghticoke Road | R | 4.4 | |
| | | 138.7 | Side trail to Bulls Bridge Road Parking Area (R 0.2m E; M 0.4m E) | RM | 3.7 | |
| | | 139.3 | Stream | w | 3.1 | |
| | | 139.4 | Ten Mile River (280') | C(nw) | 3.0 | |
| | | 139.6 | Ten Mile River Shelter | S(nw) | 2.8 | |
| | | 140.6 | Ten Mile Hill (1,000') | | 1.8 | |
| | | 141.7 | CT-55 | R | 0.7 | |
| | | 142.4 | Hoyt Road, Connecticut–New York Line (400'); **Wingdale, NY, P.O. 12594** (P.O.,G,M 3.3m W; M 1.5m W, 2.3m W) | RGM | 0.0 | |

| Club | GBS | NtoS | Features | Facilities (see page 14 for codes) | StoN | Map |
|---|---|---|---|---|---|---|
| | | *Miles from CT-NY line* | | | *Miles from Delaware Water Gap, PA* | |
| New York-New Jersey Trail Conference | NY Section 2 | 0.0 | Hoyt Road, Connecticut–New York Line (400'); **Wingdale, NY, P.O. 12594** (P.O.,G,M 3.3m W; M 1.5m W) | RGM | 163.7 | NY-NJ Map 1 |
| | | 1.0 | Duell Hollow Road | R | 162.7 | |
| | | 1.2 | Wiley Shelter | S(nw) | 162.5 | |
| | | 1.6 | Leather Hill Road (750') | R | 162.1 | |
| | | 6.7 | Hurds Corners Road | R | 157.0 | |
| | NY Section 3 | 6.9 | NY-22, Metro-North Railroad, Appalachian Trail Railroad Station (480') (G 0.6m E; L 2.6m W; M 2.4m W) | RGLM | 156.8 | |
| | | 9.3 | County 20 (West Dover Road); **Pawling, NY, P.O. 12564** (P.O.,G,M 3.1m W; C 3.1m E) | ★ RCGM | 154.4 | |
| | | 10.0 | Telephone Pioneers Shelter | Sw | 153.7 | |
| | | 10.3 | West Mountain (1,200') | | 153.4 | |
| | NY Section 4 | 14.5 | NY-55 (720'); **Poughquag, NY, P.O. 12570** (P.O.,M 3.1m W; G 3.6m W; M 1.5m W; L 2.6m W) | RGLM | 149.2 | |
| | | 14.8 | Old Route 55 | R | 148.9 | |
| | | 16.7 | Depot Hill Road | R | 147.0 | |
| | | 17.8 | Morgan Stewart Shelter | Sw | 145.9 | |
| | | 17.9 | Mt. Egbert (1,329') | | 145.8 | |
| | | 20.3 | Stormville Mountain Road, I-84 | R | 143.4 | |
| | NY Section 5 | 21.7 | NY-52 (800'); **Stormville, NY, P.O. 12582** (P.O. 1.7m W; G 2.2m W, 2.4m W; G,M 0.5m E, 2m E) | RGM | 142.0 | |
| | | 23.3 | Hosner Mountain Road | R | 140.4 | |

# New York–New Jersey

| Club | GBS | NtoS<br>Miles from CT-NY line | Features | Facilities (see page 14 for codes) | StoN<br>Miles from Delaware Water Gap, PA | Map |
|---|---|---|---|---|---|---|
| New York-New Jersey Trail Conference | NY Section 6 | 26.5 | Taconic State Parkway | R | 137.2 | NY-NJ Map 1 |
| | | 26.8 | Hortontown Road, RPH Shelter (350') | RS(nw) | 136.9 | |
| | | 28.1 | Shenandoah Tenting Area | C(nw) | 135.6 | |
| | | 29.2 | Long Hill Road | R | 134.5 | |
| | | 29.6 | Shenandoah Mountain (1,282') | | 134.1 | |
| | | 31.8 | Raymond Torrey Memorial Shelter | | 131.9 | |
| | | | (S 0.6m E) | S | | |
| | NY Section 7 | 33.8 | NY-301, Canopus Lake, | | | |
| | | | Fahnestock State Park (C,w 1m E) | RCw | 129.9 | |
| | | 35.9 | Sunk Mine Road (800') | R | 127.8 | NY-NJ Map 2 |
| | | 37.5 | Dennytown Road | RCw | 126.2 | |
| | | 40.2 | South Highland Road | R | 123.5 | |
| | NY Section 8 | 41.2 | Canopus Hill Road (420') | R | 122.5 | |
| | | 42.9 | Old Albany Post Road, Chapman Road | R | 120.8 | |
| | | 43.7 | Denning Hill (900') | | 120.0 | |
| | | 45.6 | Old West Point Road, Graymoor Friary | R | 118.1 | |
| | NY Section 9 | 46.2 | US-9, NY-403 (400'); | | | |
| | | | **Peekskill, NY, P.O. 10566** | | | |
| | | | (P.O.,G,L,M 4.8m E; M 0.7m E; G on A.T.) | RGLM | 117.5 | |
| | | 49.6 | South Mountain Pass (Manitou Road) | R | 114.1 | |
| | | 49.8 | Hemlock Springs Campsite | Cw | 113.9 | |
| | | 50.8 | Camp Smith Trail, Anthony's Nose (700') | | 112.9 | |
| | | 51.5 | NY-9D | R | 112.2 | |
| | NY Section 10 | 52.2 | Bear Mountain Bridge; | | | |
| | | | **Fort Montgomery, NY, P.O., 10922** | | | |
| | | | (P.O.,G,L,M, 0.7m W) | RGLM | 111.5 | |
| | | 52.3 | Trailside Museum and Zoo (124') | | 111.4 | |
| | | 53.0 | Bear Mountain Inn, | | | |
| | | | **Bear Mountain, NY, P.O. 10911** | | | |
| | | | (P.O. 0.3m E; L,M,w on A.T.) | RLMw | 110.7 | |

# New York–New Jersey

| Club | GBS | NtoS | Features | Facilities (see page 14 for codes) | StoN | Map |
|---|---|---|---|---|---|---|
| | | *Miles from CT-NY line* | | | *Miles from Delaware Water Gap, PA* | |
| *New York-New Jersey Trail Conference* | NY Section 10 | 54.6 | Bear Mountain (1,305') | Rw | 109.1 | NY-NJ Map 2 |
| | | 57.1 | Seven Lakes Drive | R | 106.6 | |
| | | 58.1 | West Mountain Shelter (S 1.2m E) | S(nw) | 105.6 | |
| | | 59.3 | Anthony Wayne Recreation Area | w | 104.4 | |
| | | 59.5 | Palisades Interstate Parkway (500') | R | 104.2 | |
| | | 62.1 | Black Mountain (1,160') | | 101.6 | |
| | | 63.4 | William Brien Memorial Shelter | S(nw) | 100.3 | |
| | | 64.6 | Goshen Mountain | | 99.1 | |
| | | 65.4 | Seven Lakes Drive | R | 98.3 | |
| | NY Section 11 | 67.6 | Arden Valley Road (1,196') (w 0.3m E) | Rw | 96.1 | |
| | | 68.7 | Fingerboard Shelter | S(nw) | 95.0 | |
| | | 69.8 | Surebridge Mountain | | 93.9 | |
| | | 71.0 | Lemon Squeezer | | 92.7 | |
| | | 71.5 | Island Pond Outlet | w | 92.2 | |
| | | 73.0 | Arden Valley Road | R | 90.7 | |
| | | 73.1 | New York State Thruway (560') | | 90.6 | |
| | NY Section 12 | 73.3 | NY-17; Arden, NY, P.O. 10910; **Southfields, NY, P.O. 10975** (P.O. 0.7m W; P.O.,L,M 2.1m E; G 1.8m E, 5.7m E) | RGLM | 90.4 | |
| | | 74.5 | Arden Mountain (1,180') | | 89.2 | |
| | | 75.1 | Orange Turnpike (w 0.5m E) | Rw | 88.6 | |
| | | 75.8 | Little Dam Lake | | 87.9 | |
| | | 76.5 | East Mombasha Road | R | 87.2 | |
| | | 77.3 | Buchanan Mountain (1,142') | | 86.4 | |
| | | 78.2 | West Mombasha Road (G 0.6m W) | RG | 85.5 | |

# New York–New Jersey

*Miles from CT-NY line* (NtoS) · *Miles from Delaware Water Gap, PA* (StoN)

| Club | GBS | NtoS | Features | Facilities (see page 14 for codes) | StoN | Map |
|---|---|---|---|---|---|---|
| New York-New Jersey Trail Conference | NY Section 12 | 79.4 | Mombasha High Point (1,280') | | 84.3 | NY-NJ Map 2 |
| | | 81.4 | Fitzgerald Falls | w | 82.3 | |
| | | 81.7 | Lakes Road (680') | R | 82.0 | |
| | | 83.2 | Wildcat Shelter | Sw | 80.5 | |
| | | 83.5 | Cat Rocks | | 80.2 | |
| | | 84.1 | Eastern Pinnacles (1,294') | | 79.6 | |
| | NY Section 13 | 85.3 | NY-17A; Greenwood Lake, NY, P.O. 10925<br>(G 1.6m W; P.O.,G,L,M 2m E;<br>G,L,M 3.5m W) | RGLM | 78.4 | |
| | | 90.9 | Prospect Rock (1,433') | | 72.8 | NY-NJ Map 3 |
| | NJ Section 1 | 91.3 | State Line Trail, New York–New Jersey Line;<br>**Hewitt, N.J., P.O. 07421**<br>(P.O.,G,M 3.7m E) | GM | 72.4 | |
| | | 92.4 | Long House Creek | | 71.3 | |
| | | 93.5 | Long House Road (Brady Road)<br>(G,M 0.7m W) | RGM | 70.2 | |
| | | 94.9 | Warwick Turnpike (1,140')<br>(G 1.8m E, 2.7m W; L,M 0.8m W;<br>M 1.5m E) | RGLM | 68.8 | |
| | | 95.4 | Wawayanda Shelter<br>(S on A.T.; w 0.4m E) | Sw | 68.3 | |
| | | 95.6 | Wawayanda Road | R | 68.1 | |
| | | 96.2 | Iron Mountain Road Bridge | R | 67.5 | |
| | | 97.3 | Barrett Road;<br>**New Milford, NY, P.O. 10959**<br>(P.O.,G 1.8m W) | RG | 66.4 | |
| | | 99.0 | Wawayanda Mountain (1,340') | | 64.7 | |
| | NJ 2 | 100.4 | NJ-94 (450');<br>**Vernon, NJ, P.O. 07462**<br>(P.O.,G,M 2.4m E) | ★<br>RGM | 63.3 | |

# New York–New Jersey

| Club | GBS | NtoS Miles from CT-NY line | Features | Facilities (see page 14 for codes) | StoN Miles from Delaware Water Gap, PA | Map |
|---|---|---|---|---|---|---|
| New York-New Jersey Trail Conference | NJ Section 2 | 101.3 | Canal Road | R | 62.4 | NY-NJ Map 3 |
| | | 102.0 | Pochuck Creek footbridge | | 61.7 | |
| | | 102.7 | County 517 | R | 61.0 | |
| | | 104.2 | County 565; **Glenwood, NJ, P.O. 07418** (P.O. 0.7m W; L 1m W) | RL | 59.5 | |
| | | 105.4 | Pochuck Mountain (800') | | 58.3 | |
| | | 106.9 | Pochuck Mountain Shelter | S(nw) | 56.8 | |
| | | 107.4 | Lake Wallkill Road (Liberty Corners Road) | Rw | 56.3 | |
| | | 109.7 | Wallkill River | R | 54.0 | |
| | | 110.7 | Oil City Road | R | 53.0 | |
| | | 111.2 | NJ-284 (420') (G 0.4m W) | RG | 52.5 | |
| | NJ Section 3 | 112.2 | Lott Road; Unionville, NY, P.O. 10988 (P.O.,G,M 0.4m W) | RGM | 51.5 | |
| | | 113.1 | Unionville Road | R | 50.6 | |
| | | 115.4 | Gemmer Road | R | 48.3 | |
| | | 118.0 | County 519 | R | 45.7 | |
| | | 119.3 | High Point Shelter | Sw | 44.4 | |
| | | 119.8 | Side trail to High Point Monument | | 43.9 | |
| | | 121.0 | NJ-23 (1,500') (w on A.T.; G 2.5m E, 4.3m W; L 1.4m E, 4.4m W; M 4.3m W) | RGLMw | 42.7 | |
| | NJ Section 4 | 123.9 | Trail to Rutherford Shelter (S,w 0.4m E) | Sw | 39.8 | |
| | | 126.3 | Deckertown Turnpike | R | 37.4 | |
| | | 126.5 | Mashipacong Shelter | S(nw) | 37.2 | |
| | | 129.1 | Crigger Road | R | 34.6 | |
| | | 129.9 | Sunrise Mountain (1,653') | R | 33.8 | |
| | | 132.3 | Trail to Gren Anderson Shelter | Sw | 31.4 | |

# New York–New Jersey

| Club | GBS | NtoS | Features | Facilities (see page 14 for codes) | StoN | Map |
|---|---|---|---|---|---|---|
| | | *Miles from CT-NY line* | | | *Miles from Delaware Water Gap, PA* | |
| New York-New Jersey Trail Conference | | 133.4 | Culver Fire Tower | | 30.3 | NY-NJ Map 4 |
| | NJ Section 5 | 135.4 | Culvers Gap, US-206 (935'); **Branchville, NJ, P.O. 07826** (P.O. 3.4m E; G on A.T., 1.6m E; L 2.5m E, 1.9m W; M 0.1m W, 0.6m E) | RGLM | 28.3 | |
| | | 139.0 | Brink Road Shelter (S,w 0.2m W) | Sw | 24.7 | |
| | | 141.2 | Rattlesnake Mountain (1,492') | | 22.5 | |
| | | 143.0 | Buttermilk Falls Trail | | 20.7 | |
| | | 146.0 | Blue Mountain Lakes Road | Rw | 17.7 | |
| | NJ Section 6 | 149.9 | Millbrook–Blairstown Road (1,260') | R | 13.8 | |
| | | 150.3 | Rattlesnake Spring | w | 13.4 | |
| | | 150.9 | Catfish Fire Tower (1,565') | | 12.8 | |
| | | 153.3 | Camp Mohican Road, Mohican Outdoor Center (C,L,w 0.3m W) | RCLw | 10.4 | |
| | | 157.7 | Garvey Springs Trail | w | 6.0 | |
| | | 157.8 | Sunfish Pond (1,382') | | 5.9 | |
| | | 159.1 | Backpacker Site | C(nw) | 4.6 | |
| | | 160.7 | Holly Spring Trail (w 0.2m E) | w | 3.0 | |
| | | 162.3 | I-80 Overpass | R | 1.4 | |
| | | 162.6 | Delaware Water Gap National Recreation Area Information Center | Rw | 1.1 | |
| | | 163.7 | Delaware River Bridge (west end), New Jersey–Pennsylvania Line (350') | R | 0.0 | |

# Pennsylvania

| Club | GBS | NtoS | Features | Facilities (see page 14 for codes) | StoN | Map |
|---|---|---|---|---|---|---|
| | | *Miles from Delware Water Gap, PA* | | | *Miles from PA-MD line* | |
| AMC Deleware Valley Chapter | PA Section 1 | 0.0 | Delaware River Bridge (west end), New Jersey–Pennsylvania Line (350') | R | 230.0 | KTA Sections 1-6 Map |
| | | 0.2 | PA-611, **Delaware Water Gap, PA, P.O. 18327** (P.O.,M 0.1m W; L,M 0.4m W; G,L 3.2m W) | ★ RGLM | 229.8 | |
| | | 0.9 | Council Rock | | 229.1 | |
| | | 1.7 | Lookout Rock | | 228.3 | |
| | | 2.7 | Mt. Minsi (1,461') | | 227.3 | |
| | | 4.7 | Totts Gap | | 225.3 | |
| | | 6.6 | Kirkridge Shelter (1,500') | S(w) | 223.4 | |
| | | 7.2 | Fox Gap, PA-191 | R | 222.8 | |
| Batona | | 8.5 | Wolf Rocks Bypass Trail (north end) | | 221.5 | |
| | | 8.8 | Wolf Rocks | | 221.2 | |
| | | 9.3 | Wolf Rocks Bypass Trail (south end) | | 220.7 | |
| AMC Deleware Valley Chapter | PA Section 2 | 15.7 | PA-33 (980'); **Wind Gap, PA, P.O. 18091** (P.O.,G,M 1m E; L 0.1m W) | ★ RGLM | 214.3 | |
| | | 16.7 | Hahns Lookout | | 213.3 | |
| | | 20.3 | Leroy A. Smith Shelter (S 0.1m E; w 0.2m E) | Sw | 209.7 | |
| | | 23.8 | Smith Gap Road, Point Phillips Road (W 0.6m E) | Rw | 206.2 | |
| | | 26.3 | Delps Trail (1,580') | | 203.7 | |
| Keystone Trails Assoc. | | 31.1 | Little Gap (1,100'); **Danielsville, PA, P.O. 18038** (P.O.,G,M 1.5m E; w 1.2m W) | RGMw | 198.9 | |
| | | 35.4 | Winter Trail (north junction) | | 194.6 | |
| | | 36.2 | Winter Trail (south junction) | | 193.8 | |
| | | 36.4 | PA-248 | R | 193.6 | |

# Pennsylvania

| Club | GBS | NtoS | Features | Facilities (see page 14 for codes) | StoN | Map |
|---|---|---|---|---|---|---|
| | | *Miles from Delware Water Gap, PA* | | | *Miles from PA-MD line* | |
| Keystone Trails Association | PA Section 2 | 36.6 | Lehigh River Bridge (east end), PA-873 (380');<br>**Palmerton, PA, P.O. 18071**<br>(P.O.,G,L,M 2m W) | RGLM | 193.4 | KTA Sections 1-6 Map |
| | PA Section 3 | 36.7 | Lehigh Gap, PA-873;<br>**Slatington, PA, P.O. 18080**<br>(P.O.,G,L,M 2m E) | RGLM | 193.3 | |
| | | 37.3 | George W. Outerbridge Shelter | Sw | 192.7 | |
| Blue Mtn. Eagle | | 42.4 | Ashfield Road, Blue Mountain Road<br>Lehigh Furnace Gap (1,320');<br>**Ashfield, PA, P.O. 18212**<br>(P.O.,G 2.2m W; w 0.7m E) | RGw | 187.6 | |
| | | 44.8 | Bake Oven Knob Shelter | Sw | 185.2 | |
| Allentown Hiking Club | | 45.4 | Bake Oven Knob (1,560') | | 184.6 | |
| | | 45.8 | Bake Oven Knob Road | R | 184.2 | |
| | | 47.2 | Bear Rocks | | 182.8 | |
| | | 47.9 | Knife Edge | | 182.1 | |
| | | 48.9 | New Tripoli Campsite (C,w 0.2m W) | Cw | 181.1 | |
| | PA Section 4 | 50.7 | PA-309, Blue Mountain Summit (1,360')<br>(L,M,w on A.T.) | RLMw | 179.3 | |
| | | 52.9 | Fort Franklin Road,<br>Blue Mountain House Road | R | 177.1 | |
| | | 54.8 | Allentown Hiking Club Shelter | Sw | 175.2 | |
| Blue Mtn. Eagle Climb Club | | 56.1 | Tri-County Corner (1,560') | | 173.9 | |
| | | 62.2 | Hawk Mountain Road,<br>Eckville Shelter (600')<br>(S,w 0.2m E) | RSw | 167.8 | |
| | | 67.5 | The Pinnacle | | 162.5 | |
| | | 67.9 | Trail to Blue Rocks Campground<br>(C,G,S 1.5m E) | CGS | 162.1 | |

# Pennsylvania

| Club | GBS | NtoS | Features | Facilities (see page 14 for codes) | StoN | Map |
|---|---|---|---|---|---|---|
| | | *Miles from Delware Water Gap, PA* | | | *Miles from PA-MD line* | |
| *Blue Mountain Eagle Climbing Club* | PA Section 4 | 69.7 | Pulpit Rock (1,582') | | 160.3 | KTA Sections 1-6 Map |
| | | 71.3 | Windsor Furnace Shelter (940') | Sw | 158.7 | |
| | | 71.5 | Windsor Furnace | | 158.5 | |
| | | 74.1 | Pocahontas Spring (1,200')<br>(w on A.T.; L,M 1m E) | LMw | 155.9 | |
| | | 76.7 | PA-61<br>(M 0.5m W) | RM | 153.3 | |
| | PA Section 5 | 77.4 | **Port Clinton, PA, P.O. 19549 (400')**<br>(P.O. on A.T.; L,S 0.5m W; G,M,L 3m E) | RGLMS | 152.6 | |
| | | 81.4 | Phillip's Canyon Spring (1,500') | w | 148.6 | |
| | | 84.1 | Shartlesville Cross-Mountain Road;<br>**Shartlesville, PA, P.O. 19554**<br>(P.O.,G,L,M 3.6m E) | RGLM | 145.9 | |
| | | 86.0 | Eagle's Nest Shelter<br>(S,w 0.3m W) | Sw | 144.0 | |
| | | 86.7 | Sand Spring Trail<br>(w 0.2m E) | w | 143.3 | |
| | | 90.5 | Black Swatara Spring<br>(w 0.3m E) | w | 139.5 | |
| | PA Section 6 | 91.8 | PA-183, Rentschler Marker (1,440') | R | 138.2 | |
| | | 92.1 | Fort Dietrich Snyder Marker<br>(w 0.2m W) | w | 137.9 | |
| | | 95.2 | Shuberts Gap | | 134.8 | |
| | | 95.3 | Hertlein Campsite | Cw | 134.7 | |
| | | 97.8 | Round Head and Shower Steps | w | 132.2 | |
| | | 100.4 | Trail to Pilger Ruh Spring | Cw | 129.6 | |
| | | 100.9 | PA-501; Pine Grove, PA, P.O. 17963,<br>501 Shelter<br>(P.O.,M 3.7m W; S,w 0.1m W;<br>G 4.3m W; L 5.7m W) | RGLMSw | 129.1 | |

# Pennsylvania

| Club | GBS | NtoS | Features | Facilities (see page 14 for codes) | StoN | Map |
|---|---|---|---|---|---|---|
| | | *Miles from Delware Water Gap, PA* | | | *Miles from PA-MD line* | |
| Blue Mtn. Eagle Climb Club | PA Section 6 | 102.8 | PA-645 | R | 127.2 | KTA Sect. 1-6 Map |
| | | 105.0 | Blue Mountain Spring, William Penn Shelter (1,380') | Sw | 125.0 | |
| | | 111.9 | I-81 | R | 118.1 | |
| | PA Section 7 | 112.3 | Swatara Gap, PA-72 (480') (C,G,L,M 2m E) | RGL | 117.7 | KTA Sections 7-8 Map |
| | | 113.7 | PA-443; Green Point, PA | R | 116.3 | |
| Susquehanna A.T. Club | | 118.4 | Rausch Gap Shelter (980') (S,w 0.3m E) | Sw | 111.6 | |
| | | 120.8 | Cold Spring Trail | | 109.2 | |
| | | 123.0 | Yellow Springs Village Site | | 107.0 | |
| | | 123.5 | Yellow Springs Trail | | 106.5 | |
| | | 126.5 | Stony Mountain; Horse-Shoe Trail (1,650') | | 103.5 | |
| | PA Section 8 | 129.7 | PA-325, Clarks Valley (550') | Rw | 100.3 | |
| | | 130.0 | Spring | w | 100.0 | |
| | | 132.3 | Shikellimy Trail | | 97.7 | |
| | | 133.7 | Kinter View (1,320') | | 96.3 | |
| | | 134.8 | Whitetail Trail | | 95.2 | |
| | | 135.4 | Victoria Trail | | 94.6 | |
| | | 136.4 | Peters Mountain Shelter | Sw | 93.6 | |
| | | 137.2 | Table Rock | | 92.8 | |
| York HC | | 139.2 | PA-225 | R | 90.8 | |
| | | 143.1 | Clarks Ferry Shelter (1,260') | Sw | 86.9 | |
| | | 143.3 | Campsite | Cw | 86.7 | |
| | | 145.5 | US-22 & US-322, Norfolk Southern Railway | R | 84.5 | |
| Mtn. Club of MD | PA Section 9 | 146.1 | Clarks Ferry Bridge (west end), Susquehanna River (380') (C on A.T.; M 0.1m W) | RCM | 83.9 | PATC Map 1 |
| | | 146.3 | Juniata River, PA 849 | R | 83.7 | |
| | | 147.3 | **Duncannon, PA, P.O. 17020** (P.O.,L,M on A.T., G 0.6m W) | RGLM | 82.7 | |

# Pennsylvania

| Club | GBS | NtoS | Features | Facilities (see page 14 for codes) | StoN | Map |
|---|---|---|---|---|---|---|
| | | *Miles from Delware Water Gap, PA* | | | *Miles from PA-MD line* | |
| Mtn. Club of MD | PA Section 9 | 147.8 | US-11 & US-15, PA-274 | R | 82.2 | PATC Map 1 |
| | | 149.5 | Hawk Rock | | 80.5 | |
| | | 151.4 | Cove Mountain Shelter (1,200') | Sw | 78.6 | |
| | | 156.4 | PA-850 (650') | R | 73.6 | |
| | | 158.7 | Darlington Shelter (1,250') | Sw | 71.3 | |
| Cumberland Valley A.T. Club | | 158.8 | Darlington Trail, Tuscarora Trail | | 71.2 | |
| | | 159.7 | Spring | w | 70.3 | |
| | PA Section 10 | 160.7 | PA-944 (480'); Donnellytown, PA | R | 69.3 | |
| | | 161.6 | Sherwood Drive | Rw | 68.4 | |
| | | 162.7 | Conodoguinet Creek, Scott Farm Trail Work Center | R | 67.3 | |
| | | 164.1 | I-81 Crossing | R | 65.9 | |
| | | 165.0 | US-11; Carlisle, PA, P.O. 17013 **New Kingston, PA, P.O. 17072** (P.O. 5m W; 1.7m E; G 1.3m E; L,M 0.3m W; M 0.3m E) | RGLM | 65.0 | |
| | | 166.2 | Pennsylvania Turnpike | R | 63.8 | |
| | | 168.9 | Trindle Road (PA-641) | R | 61.1 | |
| | | 171.0 | PA-74 | R | 59.0 | |
| | PA Section 11 | 173.0 | PA-174, **Boiling Springs, PA, P.O. 17007** (P.O.,w on A.T.; G,L,M 0.1m W; G 1m W) | ★ RGLMw | 57.0 | |
| | | 173.3 | Yellow Breeches Creek (500') | R | 56.7 | |
| | | 173.5 | Backpackers' Campsite | Cw | 56.5 | |
| Mtn. Club of MD | | 176.0 | Center Point Knob (1,060') | | 54.0 | |
| | | 176.9 | Alec Kennedy Shelter | Sw | 53.1 | |
| | | 179.0 | Whiskey Spring, Whiskey Spring Road | Rw | 51.0 | |
| | | 181.8 | PA-94 (880'); **Mount Holly Springs, PA, P.O. 17065** (P.O.,G,M 2.5m W) | RGM | 48.2 | |

# Pennsylvania

| Club | GBS | NtoS | Features | Facilities (see page 14 for codes) | StoN | Map |
|---|---|---|---|---|---|---|
| | | *Miles from Delware Water Gap, PA* | | | *Miles from PA-MD line* | |
| Mtn. Club of Maryland | PA Section 11 | 183.6 | Hunters Run Road (PA-34); **Gardners, PA, P.O. 17324** (P.O. 5m E; G 0.2m E) | RG | 46.4 | PATC Maps 2-3 |
| | | 184.5 | Pine Grove Road (C,M 0.4m W) | RCM | 45.5 | |
| | | 185.0 | James Fry (Tagg Run) Shelter (S,w 0.2m E) | Sw | 45.0 | |
| | | 186.2 | Side trail to Mountain Creek Campground (C,G 0.7m W) | CG | 43.8 | |
| | | 186.4 | Limekiln Road | R | 43.6 | |
| | | 189.7 | Side trail to Pole Steeple (1,300') | | 40.3 | |
| | | 192.2 | Pine Grove Furnace State Park | RCGLw | 37.8 | |
| Potomac A.T. Club | PA Section 13 | 192.5 | PA-233 (900'), Appalachian Trail Museum | R | 37.5 | |
| | | 195.9 | Toms Run Shelter | Sw | 34.1 | |
| | | 197.0 | Woodrow Road | R | 33.0 | |
| | | 198.9 | Michener Cabin (locked) (w 0.3m E) | w | 31.1 | |
| | | 200.8 | Shippensburg Road (2,040') | R | 29.2 | |
| | | 202.1 | Birch Run Shelter | Sw | 27.9 | |
| | | 204.5 | Milesburn Road, Milesburn Cabin (locked) | Rw | 25.5 | |
| | | 204.9 | Ridge Road, Means Hollow Road | R | 25.1 | |
| | | 205.4 | Middle Ridge Road | R | 24.6 | |
| | | 208.0 | Sandy Sod Junction (1,980') | R | 22.0 | |
| | | 209.5 | Quarry Gap Shelters | Sw | 20.5 | |
| | | 210.2 | Quarry Gap Road | R | 19.8 | |
| | PA Section 14 | 212.1 | US-30, Caledonia State Park, Thaddeus Stevens Museum (960'); **Fayetteville, PA, P.O. 17222** (P.O 3.9m W; C,w on A.T.; G 2.3m W; M 0.4m W; L 0.8mW) | RCGLMw | 17.9 | |

# Pennsylvania

| Club | GBS | NtoS | Features | Facilities (see page 14 for codes) | StoN | Map |
|---|---|---|---|---|---|---|
| | | *Miles from Delware Water Gap, PA* | | | *Miles from PA-MD line* | |
| Potomac A.T. Club | PA Section 14 | 215.1 | Rocky Mountain Shelters (S 0.2m E; w 0.5m E) | Sw | 14.9 | PATC Map 4 |
| | | 216.8 | PA-233 (1,600'); **South Mountain, PA, P.O. 17261** (P.O.,C,G,M 1.3m E) | RCGM | 13.2 | |
| | | 217.1 | Swamp Road | R | 12.9 | |
| | | 220.4 | Chimney Rocks (1,900') | | 9.6 | |
| | | 221.7 | Tumbling Run Shelters, Hermitage Cabin (locked) | Sw | 8.3 | |
| | | 221.9 | Old Forge Road (1,000') | R | 8.1 | |
| | | 222.5 | Rattlesnake Run Road | R | 7.5 | |
| | | 222.9 | Old Forge Park | RCw | 7.1 | |
| | | 225.3 | Deer Lick Shelters (1,420') | Sw | 4.7 | |
| | | 226.6 | Bailey Spring | w | 3.4 | |
| | | 227.2 | Mackie Run, Mentzer Gap Road | R | 2.8 | |
| | | 227.4 | PA-16; **Blue Ridge Summit, PA, P.O. 17214** (P.O.,G,M 1.3m E) | RGM | 2.6 | |
| | | | **Rouzerville, PA, P.O. 17250** (P.O.,G,L,M 2.2m W) | RGLM | 2.6 | |
| | | | **Waynesboro, PA P.O. 17268** (P.O.,G,L,M 5.7m W) | RGLM | 2.6 | |
| | | 227.7 | Old PA-16 | R | 2.3 | |
| | | 228.9 | Buena Vista Road | Rw | 1.1 | |
| | | 229.9 | Pen Mar Road | R | 0.1 | |
| | | 230.0 | Pennsylvania–Maryland Line (1,250') | R | 0.0 | |

# Maryland–West Virginia–Northern Virginia

| Club | GBS | NtoS *Miles from PA-MD line* | Features | Facilities (see page 14 for codes) | StoN *Miles from Front Royal, VA* | Map |
|---|---|---|---|---|---|---|
| *Potomac A.T. Club* | MD Section 1 | 0.0 | Pennsylvania–Maryland Line (1,250') | R | 95.2 | PATC Maps 5-6 |
| | | 0.2 | Pen Mar Park; **Cascade, MD, P.O. 21719** (P.O.,G,M 1.6m E; w on A.T.; M 1.4m E) | RGMw | 95.0 | |
| | | 3.1 | Trail to High Rock | R | 92.1 | |
| | | 4.9 | Raven Rocks Shelter (C,S 0.2m W; w 0.1m E) | CSw | 90.3 | |
| | MD Section 2 | 5.9 | Raven Rock Hollow, MD-491 | R | 89.3 | |
| | | 6.7 | Warner Gap Road | Rw | 88.5 | |
| | | 8.5 | Foxville Road (MD-77) | R | 86.7 | |
| | | 9.8 | Ensign Cowall Shelter | Sw | 85.4 | |
| | MD Section 3 | 10.0 | Wolfsville Road (MD-17) (1,400'); **Smithsburg, MD, P.O. 21783** (P.O.,G,M 2.4m W; L 6.4m W) | RGLM | 85.2 | |
| | | 14.8 | Pogo Memorial Campsite | Cw | 80.4 | |
| | | 15.4 | Black Rock Cliffs (1,800') | | 79.8 | |
| | | 16.4 | Trail to Annapolis Rock (C 0.2m W; w 0.4m W) | Cw | 78.8 | |
| | | 18.0 | Pine Knob Shelter | CSw | 77.2 | |
| | MD Section 4 | 18.6 | I-70 Footbridge, US-40 (C 1.4m W; M,w 0.5m W) | RCMw | 76.6 | |
| | | 19.4 | Boonsboro Mountain Road | R | 75.8 | |
| | | 21.5 | Washington Monument | | 73.7 | |
| | | 21.9 | Washington Monument Road | Rw | 73.3 | |
| | | 22.1 | Monument Road | R | 73.1 | |
| | MD Sect. 5 | 23.5 | Turners Gap, US Alt. 40 (1,000'); **Boonsboro, MD, P.O. 21713** ★ (M on A.T; P.O.,M 2.3m W; G 1.6m W, 3.7m W) | RGM | 71.7 | |

# Maryland–West Virginia–Northern Virginia

| Club | GBS | NtoS | Features | Facilities (see page 14 for codes) | StoN | Map |
|---|---|---|---|---|---|---|
| | | *Miles from PA-MD line* | | | *Miles from Front Royal, VA* | |
| Potomac A.T. Club | MD Section 5 | 23.7 | Dahlgren Back Pack Campground | Cw | 71.5 | PATC Maps 5-6 |
| | | 24.5 | Reno Monument Road | R | 70.7 | |
| | | 25.5 | Rocky Run Shelter (C,S,w 0.2m W) | CSw | 69.7 | |
| | | 27.1 | Lambs Knoll (1,600') | | 68.1 | |
| | | 27.3 | White Rocks Cliff | | 67.9 | |
| | | 27.9 | Trail to Bear Spring Cabin (locked) (w 0.5m E) | w | 67.3 | |
| | | 30.5 | Crampton Gap Shelter (C,S,w 0.3m E) | CSw | 64.7 | |
| | MD Section 6 | 30.9 | Crampton Gap, Gathland State Park, Gapland Road (MD 572) (950'); **Burkittsville, MD, P.O. 21718** (P.O. 1.2m E; w on A.T.) | Rw | 64.3 | |
| | | 32.6 | Brownsville Gap | | 62.6 | |
| | | 34.6 | Ed Garvey Shelter (S on A.T.; w 0.4m E) | Sw | 60.6 | |
| | | 36.7 | Trail to Weverton Cliffs | | 58.5 | |
| | MD Section 7 | 37.6 | Weverton Road (G 1.4m W) | RG | 57.6 | |
| | | 37.8 | US-340 Underpass | | 57.4 | |
| | | 38.0 | Keep Tryst Road (L,M 1.2m W) | RLM | 57.2 | |
| | | 38.1 | C&O Canal Towpath (east junction) | | 57.1 | |
| | | 39.6 | US-340, Sandy Hook Bridge | | 55.6 | |
| | | 40.7 | C&O Canal Towpath (west junction) | | 54.5 | |
| | | 40.9 | Potomac River, Goodloe Byron Memorial Footbridge, Maryland–West Virginia Line (250') | | 54.3 | |

# Maryland–West Virginia–Northern Virginia

Club | GBS | NtoS | Features | Facilities (see page 14 for codes) | StoN | Map

| Club | GBS | NtoS *Miles from PA-MD line* | Features | Facilities | StoN *Miles from Front Royal, VA* | Map |
|---|---|---|---|---|---|---|
| Potomac A.T. Club | WV-VA Section 1 | 41.0 | Shenandoah Street; Harpers Ferry National Historical Park (M 0.1m W) | RM | 54.2 | PATC Map 7 |
| | | 41.6 | Appalachian Trail Conservancy Side Trail; **Harpers Ferry, WV, P.O. 25425** (P.O. 0.5m W; G 1.1m W; L 0.6m W; M 0.4m W; ATC 0.2m W) | ★ RGLM | 53.6 | |
| | | 41.9 | US-340, Shenandoah River Bridge (north end) (L 0.1m W; C 1.2m W) | RCL | 53.3 | |
| | | 42.6 | Chestnut Hill Road (WV-32) | R | 52.6 | |
| | | 43.1 | Loudoun Heights Trail to Split Rock | | 52.1 | |
| | | 43.3 | West Virginia–Virginia Line (1,200') | | 51.9 | |
| | | 45.6 | Four Mile Campsite | C(nw) | 49.6 | |
| | | 47.5 | Keys Gap, WV-9 (G,M,w 0.3m W, 0.3m E) | RGMw | 47.7 | |
| | WV-VA Section 2 | 50.5 | David Lesser Memorial Shelter (S 0.1m E; C,w 0.3m E) | CSw | 44.7 | |
| | | 53.7 | Trail to Blackburn Trail Center (1,650') (C 0.1m E; S,w 0.3m E) | CSw | 41.5 | |
| | | 54.9 | Wilson Gap | | 40.3 | |
| | | 57.8 | Devils Racecourse | | 37.4 | |
| | | 57.9 | Sand Spring | w | 37.3 | |
| | | 58.5 | Crescent Rock | | 36.7 | |
| | | 58.6 | West Virginia–Virginia Line | | 36.6 | |
| | | 58.9 | Spring | w | 36.3 | |
| | VA Sect. 3 | 61.1 | Snickers Gap, VA-7, VA-679 (1,000'); **Bluemont, VA, P.O. 20135** (P.O. 1.7m E; G 1m W; M 0.3m W, 0.9m W) | ★ RGM | 34.1 | |

# Maryland–West Virginia–Northern Virginia

| Club | GBS | NtoS | Features | Facilities (see page 14 for codes) | StoN | Map |
|---|---|---|---|---|---|---|
| | | *Miles from PA-MD line* | | | *Miles from Front Royal, VA* | |
| Potomac A.T. Club | VA Section 3 | 61.7 | Bears Den Rocks, Bears Den Hostel (L,w 0.2m E) | Lw | 33.5 | PATC Map 8 |
| | | 64.7 | Sawmill Spring, Sam Moore Shelter | Sw | 30.5 | |
| | | 66.7 | Spring | w | 28.5 | |
| | | 67.9 | Morgans Mill Road (VA-605) | R | 27.3 | |
| | | 71.1 | Fisher Loop Trail (north junction) | | 24.1 | |
| | | 71.6 | Rod Hollow Shelter | Sw | 23.6 | |
| | | 71.9 | Fisher Loop Trail (south junction) | | 23.3 | |
| | VA Section 4 | 75.2 | Ashby Gap, US-50 (900') (G,M 0.8m W; L 4m W; L,M 1.2m E) | RLM | 20.0 | |
| | | 77.8 | Sky Meadows State Park Side Trail (C,w 1.3m E) | Cw | 17.4 | |
| | | 79.0 | Spring | w | 16.2 | |
| | | 80.0 | Whiskey Hollow Shelter (S,w 0.2m E) | Sw | 15.2 | |
| | | 82.6 | Trillium Trail (1,900') | | 12.6 | |
| | | 84.5 | Manassas Gap Shelter | Sw | 10.7 | |
| | VA Section 5 | 87.0 | VA-55 (800'); Linden, VA, P.O. 22642 (P.O.,G 1m W) | RG | 8.2 | |
| | | 88.9 | VA-638 | R | 6.3 | |
| | | 90.0 | Jim & Molly Denton Shelter | CSw | 5.2 | |
| | | 91.9 | Mosby Campsite, Tom Sealock Spring (1,800') | Cw | 3.3 | |
| | | 95.2 | US-522 (950'); **Front Royal, VA, P.O. 22630** (P.O.,G 4.2m W; G,M 3.2m W; L,M 3.6m W) | ★ RGLM | 0.0 | |

# Shenandoah National Park

| Club | GBS | NtoS | Features | Facilities (see page 14 for codes) | StoN | Map |
|---|---|---|---|---|---|---|
| | | *Miles from Front Royal, VA* | | | *Miles from Rockfish Gap, VA* | |
| Potomac A.T. Club | SNP Section 1 (VA 6) | 0.0 | US-522 (950'); **Front Royal, VA, P.O. 22630** (P.O.,G 4.2m W; G,M 3.2m W; L,M 3.6m W) | ★ RGLM | 107.8 | PATC Map 9 |
| | | 1.4 | VA-602 | R | 106.4 | |
| | | 2.9 | Tom Floyd Wayside | Sw | 104.9 | |
| | | 3.6 | Possums Rest Overlook, SNP northern boundary; self-registration station for SNP camping permits | | 104.2 | |
| | | 3.8 | Compton Gap Horse Trail | | 104.0 | |
| | | 5.3 | Indian Run Spring (w 0.3m E) | w | 102.5 | |
| | | 5.6 | Compton Gap; Skyline Drive, mile 10.4 | R | 102.2 | |
| | | 6.4 | Compton Peak (2,909') | | 101.4 | |
| | | 6.8 | Compton Springs | w | 101.0 | |
| | | 7.7 | Jenkins Gap; Skyline Drive, mile 12.3 | R | 100.1 | |
| | | 9.4 | Hogwallow Gap; Skyline Drive, mile 14.2 (2,739') | R | 98.4 | |
| | | 10.0 | Hogwallow Spring | w | 97.8 | |
| | | 10.9 | North Marshall Mountain (3,368') | | 96.9 | |
| | | 11.6 | Skyline Drive, mile 15.9 | R | 96.2 | |
| | | 12.1 | South Marshall Mountain (3,212') | | 95.7 | |
| | SNP Section 2 (VA 7) | 13.2 | Gravel Springs Gap; Skyline Drive, mile 17.7 (2,666') | R | 94.6 | |
| | | 13.4 | Gravel Springs Hut (S,w 0.2m E) | Sw | 94.4 | |
| | | 14.5 | Skyline Drive, mile 18.9 | R | 93.3 | |
| | | 15.0 | Little Hogback Mountain | | 92.8 | |
| | | 15.1 | Little Hogback Overlook; Skyline Drive, mile 19.7 | R | 92.7 | |

# Shenandoah National Park

| Club | GBS | NtoS | Features | Facilities (see page 14 for codes) | StoN | Map |
|---|---|---|---|---|---|---|
| | | *Miles from Front Royal, VA* | | | *Miles from Rockfish Gap, VA* | |
| Potomac A.T. Club | SNP Section 2 (VA 7) | 15.8 | First peak of Hogback | | 92.0 | PATC Map 9 |
| | | 15.9 | Spring (w 0.2m E) | w | 91.9 | |
| | | 16.1 | Second peak of Hogback (3,475') | | 91.7 | |
| | | 16.3 | Skyline Drive, mile 20.8 | R | 91.5 | |
| | | 16.4 | Third peak of Hogback | | 91.4 | |
| | | 16.6 | Skyline Drive, mile 21.1 | R | 91.2 | |
| | | 17.0 | Tuscarora Trail | | 90.8 | |
| | | 17.6 | Rattlesnake Point Overlook; Skyline Drive, mile 21.9 | R | 90.2 | |
| | | 18.3 | Range View Cabin (locked) (w 0.1m E) | w | 89.5 | |
| | | 19.1 | Elkwallow Gap; Skyline Drive, mile 23.9 (2,480') (G,M 0.1m E) | RGM | 88.7 | |
| | | 19.6 | Spring | w | 88.2 | |
| | | 24.2 | Byrds Nest #4 Picnic Shelter (0.5m E) | w | 83.6 | |
| | | 24.3 | Beahms Gap; Skyline Drive, mile 28.5 | R | 83.5 | |
| | | 24.6 | Skyline Drive, mile 28.6 | R | 83.2 | |
| | | 25.7 | Pass Mountain (3,052') | | 82.1 | |
| | | 26.5 | Pass Mountain Hut (S,w 0.2m E) | Sw | 81.3 | |
| | SNP Section 3 (VA 8) | 27.7 | Thornton Gap, US-211; Skyline Drive, mile 31.5 (2,307') | R | 80.1 | PATC Map 10 |
| | | 29.6 | Marys Rock (3,514') | | 78.2 | |
| | | 30.2 | Meadow Spring (w 0.3m E) | w | 77.6 | |
| | | 30.9 | Byrds Nest #3 Shelter (w 0.3m E) | S | 76.9 | |
| | | 31.9 | The Pinnacle (3,730') | | 75.9 | |

# Shenandoah National Park

| Club | GBS | NtoS | Features | Facilities (see page 14 for codes) | StoN | Map |
|---|---|---|---|---|---|---|
| | | *Miles from Front Royal, VA* | | | *Miles from Rockfish Gap, VA* | |
| Potomac A.T. Club | SNP Section 3 (VA 8) | 32.9 | Side trail to Jewell Hollow Overlook; Skyline Drive, mile 36.4 | R | 74.9 | PATC Map 10 |
| | | 33.0 | Pinnacles Picnic Ground; Skyline Drive, mile 36.7 | Rw | 74.8 | |
| | | 35.2 | Hughes River Gap; side trail to Stony Man Mountain Overlook; Skyline Drive, mile 38.6 (3,097') | Rw | 72.6 | |
| | | 36.8 | Side trail to Stony Man summit | | 71.0 | |
| | SNP Section 4 (VA 9) | 37.2 | Skyland Service Road (north) (L,M 0.3m W) | RLM | 70.6 | |
| | | 38.0 | Skyland Service Road (south) | R | 69.8 | |
| | | 40.1 | Side trail to Crescent Rock Overlook; Skyline Drive, mile 44.4 | R | 67.7 | |
| | | 40.5 | Hawksbill Gap; Skyline Drive, mile 45.6 (3,361') | R | 67.3 | |
| | | 41.5 | Side trail to Hawksbill Mountain, Byrd's Nest #2 Picnic Shelter (0.9m E) | | 66.3 | |
| | | 41.8 | Rock Spring Cabin (locked) & Hut (S,w 0.2m W) | Sw | 66.0 | |
| | SNP Section 5 (VA 10) | 43.7 | Fishers Gap; Skyline Drive, mile 49.3 | R | 64.1 | |
| | | 44.7 | David Spring | w | 63.1 | |
| | | 45.3 | Big Meadows (3,500') (C,L,M 0.1m E) | RCLM | 62.5 | |
| | | 46.2 | Big Meadows Wayside, Harry F. Byrd, Sr., Visitor Center (w on A.T.; G,M 0.4m E) | RGMw | 61.6 | |
| | | 47.0 | Spring | w | 60.8 | |
| | | 47.9 | Milam Gap; Skyline Drive, mile 52.8 | R | 59.9 | |
| | | 49.8 | Hazeltop (3,812') | | 58.0 | |

# Shenandoah National Park

| Club | GBS | NtoS | Features | Facilities (see page 14 for codes) | StoN | Map |
|---|---|---|---|---|---|---|
| | | *Miles from Front Royal, VA* | | | *Miles from Rockfish Gap, VA* | |
| Potomac A.T. Club | SNP Section 5 (VA 10) | 50.7 | Bootens Gap; Skyline Drive, mile 55.1 (3,243') | R | 57.1 | PATC Map 10 |
| | | 53.3 | Bearfence Mountain Hut (S,w 0.1m E) | Sw | 54.5 | |
| | | 54.0 | Lewis Mountain Campground; Skyline Drive, mile 57.6 (C,G,L,w 0.1m W) | RCGLw | 53.8 | |
| | | 55.7 | Spring | w | 52.1 | |
| | | 56.0 | Pocosin Cabin (locked) | w | 51.8 | |
| | | 59.3 | South River Picnic Grounds (w 0.1m W) | w | 48.5 | |
| | SNP Section 6 (VA 11) | 62.3 | Swift Run Gap, US- 33; Skyline Drive, mile 65.5 (2,367') | R | 45.5 | PATC Map 11 |
| | | 63.6 | Skyline Drive, mile 66.7 | R | 44.2 | |
| | | 65.1 | Hightop Mountain (3,587') | | 42.7 | |
| | | 65.2 | Spring | w | 42.6 | |
| | | 65.7 | Hightop Hut (S 0.1m W; w 0.2m W) | Sw | 42.1 | |
| | | 66.9 | Smith Roach Gap; Skyline Drive, mile 68.6 | R | 40.9 | |
| | | 68.1 | Little Roundtop Mountain | | 39.7 | |
| | | 68.5 | Powell Gap; Skyline Drive, mile 69.9 (2,294') | R | 39.3 | |
| | SNP Section 7 (VA 12) | 71.8 | Simmons Gap; Skyline Drive, mile 73.2 | Rw | 36.0 | |
| | | 73.7 | Pinefield Gap; Skyline Drive, mile 75.2 | R | 34.1 | |
| | | 73.9 | Pinefield Hut | Sw | 33.9 | |
| | | 75.5 | Ivy Creek Overlook; Skyline Drive, mile 77.5 | R | 32.3 | |
| | | 77.6 | Spring (w 0.1m W) | w | 30.2 | |

# Shenandoah National Park

| Club | GBS | NtoS | Features | Facilities (see page 14 for codes) | StoN | Map |
|---|---|---|---|---|---|---|
| | | *Miles from Front Royal, VA* | | | *Miles from Rockfish Gap, VA* | |
| Potomac A.T. Club | SNP Section 7 (VA 12) | 79.7 | Loft Mountain Campground (3,300') (C,G,M,w 0.2m W) | CGMw | 28.1 | PATC Map 11 |
| | | 81.8 | Doyles River Cabin (locked); Skyline Drive, mile 81.1 (w 0.3m E) | Rw | 26.0 | |
| | | 82.7 | Doyles River Parking Overlook; Skyline Drive, mile 81.9 | R | 25.1 | |
| | | 83.1 | Skyline Drive, mile 82.2 | R | 24.7 | |
| | SNP Section 8 (VA 13) | 84.0 | Browns Gap; Skyline Drive, mile 82.9 (2,600') | R | 23.8 | |
| | | 85.5 | Skyline Drive, mile 84.3 | R | 22.3 | |
| | | 86.5 | Blackrock (3,100') | | 21.3 | |
| | | 87.1 | Blackrock Hut (S,w 0.2m E) | Sw | 20.7 | |
| | | 87.6 | Skyline Drive, mile 87.2 | R | 20.2 | |
| | | 87.8 | Blackrock Gap; Skyline Drive, mile 87.4 (2,321') | R | 20.0 | |
| | | 89.6 | Skyline Drive, mile 88.9 | R | 18.2 | |
| | | 93.7 | Skyline Drive, mile 92.4 (3,100') | R | 14.1 | |
| | | 95.7 | Turk Gap; Skyline Drive, mile 94.1 | R | 12.1 | |
| | | 97.3 | Skyline Drive, mile 95.3 | R | 10.5 | |
| | | 98.9 | Spring | w | 8.9 | |
| | SNP Section 9 (VA 14) | 99.1 | Jarman Gap; Skyline Drive, mile 96.9; SNP southern boundary (2,173') | R | 8.7 | |
| | | 99.5 | Spring | w | 8.3 | |
| | | 100.1 | Calf Mountain Shelter (w 0.2m W; S 0.3m W) | Sw | 7.7 | |
| | | 102.3 | Beagle Gap; Skyline Drive, mile 99.5 | R | 5.5 | |
| | | 102.8 | Bear Den Mountain (2,885') | | 5.0 | |
| | | 104.1 | McCormick Gap; Skyline Drive, mile 102.1 | R | 3.7 | |

# Shenandoah National Park

| Club | GBS | NtoS Miles from Front Royal, VA | Features | Facilities (see page 14 for codes) | StoN Miles from Rockfish Gap, VA | Map |
|---|---|---|---|---|---|---|
| Potomac A.T. Club | SNP Secti. 9 (VA 14) | 107.0 | Self-registration for SNP camping permits, park entrance station (0.2m W) | | 0.8 | PATC Map 11 |
| | | 107.5 | Skyline Drive, mile 105.2 | R | 0.3 | |
| | | 107.7 | I-64 Overpass | | 0.1 | |
| | | 107.8 | Rockfish Gap, US-250, I-64 (1,902'); **Waynesboro, VA, P.O. 22980** (P.O.,G,L,M 4.5m W; G,L,M on A.T.) | ★ RGLM | 0.0 | |

# Central Virginia

| Club | GBS | NtoS | Features | Facilities (see page 14 for codes) | StoN | Map |
|---|---|---|---|---|---|---|
| | | *Miles from Rockfish Gap, VA* | | | *Miles from New River, VA* | |
| Old Dominion A.T. Club | VA Section 15 | 0.0 | Rockfish Gap, US-250, I-64 (1,902'); **Waynesboro, VA, P.O. 22980** (P.O.,G,L,M 4.5m W) | ★ RGLM | 227.3 | Central VA Map 1 |
| | | 4.8 | Mill Creek, Paul C. Wolfe Shelter | Sw | 222.5 | |
| | | 6.1 | Jack Albright Trail | | 221.2 | |
| | | 6.5 | Side trail to Glass Hollow Overlook | | 220.8 | |
| | | 7.4 | Side trail to Humpback Rocks Visitors Center (w 0.5m W) | w | 219.9 | |
| | | 9.7 | Bear Spring | w | 217.6 | |
| | | 10.3 | Side trail to Humpback Rocks | | 217.0 | |
| | | 11.5 | Humpback Mountain (3,606') | | 215.8 | |
| | | 14.3 | Dripping Rock Parking Area; Blue Ridge Parkway, mile 9.6 | Rw | 213.0 | |
| | | 14.8 | Cedar Cliffs | | 212.5 | |
| | | 18.6 | Three Ridges Overlook; Blue Ridge Parkway, mile 13.1 | R | 208.7 | |
| Tidewater A.T. Club | VA Section 16 | 19.1 | Reids Gap (2,645'), VA-664; Blue Ridge Parkway, mile 13.6 | R | 208.2 | |
| | | 20.8 | Maupin Field Shelter | Sw | 206.5 | |
| | | 22.8 | Hanging Rock Overlook | | 204.5 | |
| | | 23.3 | Three Ridges Mountain (3,970') | | 204.0 | |
| | | 25.0 | Chimney Rocks | | 202.3 | |
| | | 27.0 | Harpers Creek Shelter | Sw | 200.3 | |
| | | 29.7 | Tye River | Cw | 197.6 | |
| NBATC | VA Section 17 | 29.8 | VA-56 (997') (C,L 4.1m W) | RCL | 197.5 | |
| | | 31.1 | Cripple Creek | w | 196.2 | |
| | | 34.1 | The Priest (4,063') | | 193.2 | |
| | | 34.6 | The Priest Shelter | Sw | 192.7 | |

# Central Virginia

Club: Natural Bridge A.T. Club (NBATC)
GBS: VA Section 17, VA Section 18, VA Section 19, VA Section 20
Map: Central VA Map 1, C. VA Map 2

| NtoS Miles from Rockfish Gap, VA | Features | Facilities (see page 14 for codes) | StoN Miles from New River, VA |
|---|---|---|---|
| 35.5 | Meadows Lane (VA-826), Crabtree Falls Trail (C,w 0.5m W; C,L 4.1m E) | RCLw | 191.8 |
| 36.3 | Cash Hollow Road (3,280'); **Montebello, VA, P.O. 24464** (P.O.,C,G,L 4.5m W) | RCGL | 191.0 |
| 37.6 | Cash Hollow Rock | | 189.7 |
| 38.4 | Spy Rock | | 188.9 |
| 38.9 | Spy Rock Road (3,454') | | 188.4 |
| 40.1 | Porters Field | Cw | 187.2 |
| 41.2 | Seeley-Woodworth Shelter | Sw | 186.1 |
| 41.9 | Elk Pond Branch | Cw | 185.4 |
| 43.1 | North Fork of Piney River | Cw | 184.2 |
| 45.0 | Greasy Spring Road | R | 182.3 |
| 45.5 | USFS-246 | R | 181.8 |
| 46.7 | Salt Log Gap (north), USFS-63 (3,290') | R | 180.6 |
| 48.0 | Tar Jacket Ridge (3,840') | | 179.3 |
| 48.9 | Hog Camp Gap, USFS-48 (3,485') | RCw | 178.4 |
| 50.2 | Cole Mountain (4,022') | | 177.1 |
| 51.4 | Old Hotel Trail, Cow Camp Gap Shelter (3,428') (S,w 0.6m E) | Sw | 175.9 |
| 52.4 | Bald Knob (4,059') | | 174.9 |
| 55.2 | Long Mountain Wayside, US-60 (2,060'); **Buena Vista, VA, P.O. 24416** (P.O.,C,G,L,M 9.3m W) | ★ RCGLM | 172.1 |
| 57.0 | Brown Mountain Creek Shelter | Sw | 170.3 |
| 59.0 | Swapping Camp Road (USFS-38) | R | 168.3 |
| 61.9 | Pedlar River Bridge | w | 165.4 |
| 62.0 | USFS-39 | R | 165.3 |

# Central Virginia

| Club | GBS | NtoS | Features | Facilities (see page 14 for codes) | StoN | Map |
|---|---|---|---|---|---|---|
| | | *Miles from Rockfish Gap, VA* | | | *Miles from New River, VA* | |
| Natural Bridge A.T. Club (NBATC) | VA Section 21 | 63.9 | Rice Mountain (2,169') | | 163.4 | Central VA Map 2 |
| | | 65.8 | Robinson Gap Road (VA-607) | R | 161.5 | |
| | | 66.1 | Blue Ridge Parkway, mile 51.7; Punchbowl Mountain Crossing (2,170') | Rw | 161.2 | |
| | | 66.5 | Punchbowl Shelter (S,w 0.2m W) | Sw | 160.8 | |
| | | 67.0 | Punchbowl Mountain | | 160.3 | |
| | | 68.1 | Bluff Mountain (3,391') | | 159.2 | |
| | | 69.6 | Saltlog Gap (south) (2,573') | | 157.7 | |
| | | 70.7 | Saddle Gap, Saddle Gap Trail | | 156.6 | |
| | | 72.2 | Big Rocky Row (2,974') | | 155.1 | |
| | | 73.2 | Fullers Rocks, Little Rocky Row (2,486') | | 154.1 | |
| | | 73.3 | Rocky Row Trail | | 154.0 | |
| | | 75.3 | Johns Hollow Shelter | Sw | 152.0 | |
| | | 75.9 | VA-812 (USFS-36) | R | 151.4 | |
| | | 76.0 | Rocky Row Run (760') | Cw | 151.3 | |
| | | 76.9 | Lower Rocky Row Run bridge | w | 150.4 | |
| | | 77.0 | US-501, VA-130; **Big Island, VA, P.O. 24526; Glasgow, VA, P.O. 24555** (P.O.,G,M 5.6m E; P.O.,C,G,L,M,S 5.9m W; C,L 4.8m E) | ★ RCGLMS | 150.3 | |
| | VA Section 22 | 77.2 | James River Foot Bridge (678') *(camping may be banned here to USFS-35)* | | 150.1 | |
| | | 78.4 | Campsite | Cw | 148.9 | |
| | | 79.2 | Matts Creek Shelter | Sw | 148.1 | |
| | | 81.1 | Big Cove Branch | w | 146.2 | |
| | | 81.9 | Sulphur Spring Trail (north crossing) (2,588') | | 145.4 | |
| | | 82.4 | Hickory Stand, Gunter Ridge Trail | | 144.9 | |

# Central Virginia

| Club | GBS | NtoS | Features | Facilities (see page 14 for codes) | StoN | Map |
|---|---|---|---|---|---|---|
| | | *Miles from Rockfish Gap, VA* | | | *Miles from New River, VA* | |
| Natural Bridge A.T. Club (NBATC) | VA Section 22 | 84.2 | Sulphur Spring Trail (south crossing) | | 143.1 | Central VA Map 2 |
| | | 84.7 | Marble Spring | Cw | 142.6 | |
| | | 85.9 | Highcock Knob (3,054')<br>*(camping may be banned here to James River)* | | 141.4 | |
| | VA Section 23 | 87.1 | Petites Gap, USFS-35;<br>Blue Ridge Parkway, mile 71.0 (2,369') | R | 140.2 | |
| | | 88.5 | Harrison Ground Spring | w | 138.8 | |
| | | 90.4 | Thunder Ridge Overlook;<br>Blue Ridge Parkway, mile 74.7 (3,525') | R | 136.9 | |
| | | 90.8 | Lower Blue Ridge Parkway<br>crossing, mile 74.9 | R | 136.5 | |
| | | 91.8 | Thunder Hill Shelter | Sw | 135.5 | |
| | | 92.1 | Upper Blue Ridge Parkway<br>crossing, mile 76.3 | R | 135.2 | |
| | | 92.7 | The Guillotine | | 134.6 | |
| | | 93.0 | Apple Orchard Mountain (4,206') | | 134.3 | |
| | VA Section 24 | 94.4 | Parkers Gap Road (USFS-812);<br>Blue Ridge Parkway, mile 78.4 (3,410') | R | 132.9 | |
| | | 94.5 | Apple Orchard Falls Trail | | 132.8 | |
| | | 96.2 | Black Rock side trail | | 131.1 | |
| | | 97.1 | Cornelius Creek Shelter | Sw | 130.2 | |
| | | 97.7 | Floyd Mountain (3,560') | | 129.6 | |
| | | 102.0 | Bryant Ridge Shelter (1,330') | Sw | 125.3 | |
| | | 104.2 | Fork Mountain (2,042') | | 123.1 | |
| | VA Section 25 | 105.8 | VA-614, Jennings Creek (987')<br>(w on A.T.; C,G,L,M 1.6m E,<br>M 4.5m W) | RCGLMw | 121.5 | |
| | | 107.3 | Buchanan Trail | | 120.0 | |
| | | 109.0 | Cove Mountain Shelter | S(nw) | 118.3 | |
| | | 110.4 | Little Cove Mountain Trail | | 116.9 | |

# Central Virginia

| Club | GBS | NtoS | Features | Facilities (see page 14 for codes) | StoN | Map |
|---|---|---|---|---|---|---|
| | | *Miles from Rockfish Gap, VA* | | | *Miles from New River, VA* | |
| *Natural Bridge A.T. Club (NBATC)* | | 110.8 | Cove Mountain (2,707') | | 116.5 | Central VA Map 2 |
| | VA Section 26 | 112.4 | Bearwallow Gap, VA-43, Blue Ridge Parkway, mile 90.9 (2,228'); **Buchanan, VA, P.O. 24066** (P.O.,G,M 5m W; M 7m W; C,L,M 4.9m E) | RCGLM | 114.9 | |
| | | 114.1 | Blue Ridge Parkway, mile 91.8; Mills Gap Overlook | R | 113.2 | |
| | | 114.8 | Blue Ridge Parkway, mile 92.5; Peaks of Otter Overlook | R | 112.5 | |
| | | 115.5 | Bobblets Gap Shelter (S,w 0.2m W) | Sw | 111.8 | Central VA Map 3 |
| | | 117.9 | Blue Ridge Parkway, mile 95.3; Harveys Knob Overlook | R | 109.4 | |
| | | 118.5 | Blue Ridge Parkway, mile 95.9; Montvale Overlook | R | 108.8 | |
| | | 119.6 | Blue Ridge Parkway, mile 97.0; Taylors Mountain Overlook | R | 107.7 | |
| *Roanoke A.T. Club* | VA Section 27 | 120.4 | Black Horse Gap, Old Fincastle Road (USFS-186); Blue Ridge Parkway, mile 97.7 (2,402') | R | 106.9 | |
| | | 122.4 | Spring | w | 104.9 | |
| | | 122.8 | Wilson Creek Shelter | Sw | 104.5 | |
| | | 123.5 | Wilson Creek | w | 103.8 | |
| | | 125.4 | Curry Creek | w | 101.9 | |
| | | 126.2 | Salt Pond Road (USFS-191) | R | 101.1 | |
| | | 129.0 | Fullhardt Knob Shelter (2,676') | Sw | 98.3 | |
| | | 132.0 | VA-652 (Mountain Pass Road) | R | 95.3 | |
| | | 132.5 | Norfolk Southern Railway, US-11; **Troutville, VA, P.O. 24175** (P.O. 0.8m W; G 1.2m W; L,M 1m E) | ★ RGLM | 94.8 | |

# Central Virginia

| Club | GBS | NtoS | Features | Facilities (see page 14 for codes) | StoN | Map |
|---|---|---|---|---|---|---|
| | | *Miles from Rockfish Gap, VA* | | | *Miles from New River, VA* | |
| Roanoke A.T. Club | VA Section 28 | 132.8 | VA-779, I-81 (L 0.1m W) | RL | 94.5 | Central VA Map 3 |
| | | 134.0 | US-220; **Daleville, VA, P.O. 24083;** (P.O. 1m W; G,L,M on A.T.) | RGLM | 93.3 | |
| | | 134.5 | Tinker Creek (1,165') | | 92.8 | |
| | | 138.0 | Hay Rock, Tinker Ridge | | 89.3 | |
| | | 139.1 | Angels Gap | | 88.2 | |
| | | 143.1 | Lamberts Meadow Campsite, Sawmill Run | Cw | 84.2 | |
| | | 143.4 | Lamberts Meadow Shelter | Sw | 83.9 | |
| | | 144.0 | Scorched Earth Gap, Andy Layne Trail | | 83.3 | |
| | | 144.5 | Tinker Cliffs (3,000') | | 82.8 | |
| | | 146.3 | Brickey's Gap | | 81.0 | |
| | | 149.4 | Campbell Shelter | Sw | 77.9 | |
| | | 149.5 | Pig Farm Campsite | Cw | 77.8 | |
| | | 150.1 | McAfee Knob (3,199') | | 77.2 | |
| | | 151.4 | Fire Road Connector Trail north junction | | 75.9 | |
| | | 151.8 | Catawba Mountain Shelter | Sw | 75.5 | |
| | | 152.8 | Johns Spring Shelter | S | 74.5 | |
| | | 153.5 | Fire Road Connector Trail south junction | | 73.8 | |
| | | 153.8 | VA-311; Catawba, VA, P.O. 24070 (P.O. 1m W) | R | 73.5 | |
| | | 154.4 | Catawba Greenway | | 72.9 | |
| | | 158.1 | VA-785 (Blacksburg Road) (1,790') | R | 69.2 | |
| | VA Section 29 | 159.7 | VA-624 (Newport Road), North Mountain Trail (G 0.4m W; L 0.4m E) | RGL | 67.6 | |
| | | 160.7 | Rawies Rest | | 66.6 | |
| | | 161.2 | Lost Spectacles Gap | | 66.1 | |
| | | 162.2 | Dragons Tooth, Cove Mountain (3,020') | | 65.1 | |

# Central Virginia

| Club | GBS | NtoS | Features | Facilities (see page 14 for codes) | StoN | Map |
|---|---|---|---|---|---|---|
| | | *Miles from Rockfish Gap, VA* | | | *Miles from New River, VA* | |
| Roanoke A.T. Club | VA Section 29 | 166.4 | Pickle Branch Shelter (S,w 0.3m E) | Sw | 60.9 | Central VA Map 3 |
| | | 167.6 | Trout Creek, VA-620 (Miller Cove Road) (1,525') | R | 59.7 | |
| | | 171.4 | Audie Murphy Monument (3,100') | | 55.9 | |
| | VA Section 30 | 175.2 | Craig Creek Valley, VA 621 (1,560') | R | 52.1 | Central VA Map 4 |
| | | 176.5 | Niday Shelter | Sw | 50.8 | |
| | | 178.9 | Sinking Creek Mountain (3,490') | | 48.4 | |
| | | 182.5 | Sarver Hollow Shelter (S,w 0.4m E) | Sw | 44.8 | |
| | | 185.8 | VA-630, Sinking Creek (2,100') | Rw | 41.5 | |
| | VA Section 31 | 186.7 | Sinking Creek Valley, VA-42 | R | 40.6 | |
| | | 189.1 | Laurel Creek Shelter | Sw | 38.2 | |
| | | 192.1 | Rocky Gap, VA-601 | R | 35.2 | |
| | | 193.1 | Stream | w | 34.2 | |
| | VA Section 32 | 194.1 | Johns Creek Valley, USFS-156 (2,102') | Rw | 33.2 | |
| | | 194.9 | War Spur Shelter | Sw | 32.4 | |
| | | 199.1 | Campsites, spring | Cw | 28.2 | |
| | | 200.3 | Wind Rock (4,121') | | 27.0 | |
| | | 200.5 | Mountain Lake Road Salt Sulphur Turnpike (VA-613) | R | 26.8 | |
| | | 204.2 | Bailey Gap Shelter | S | 23.1 | |
| | | 204.4 | Spring | w | 22.9 | |
| | | 205.7 | VA-635 (Big Stony Creek Road), Stony Creek (2,450') | R | 21.6 | |
| | | 206.7 | Dismal Branch | w | 20.6 | |
| | VA Sect. 33 | 207.8 | VA-635 (Big Stony Creek Road), Stony Creek Valley | R | 19.5 | |
| | | 208.1 | Pine Swamp Branch Shelter | Sw | 19.2 | |
| | | 210.6 | Allegheny Trail | | 16.7 | |

# Central Virginia

| Club | GBS | NtoS | Features | Facilities (see page 14 for codes) | StoN | Map |
|---|---|---|---|---|---|---|
| | | *Miles from Rockfish Gap, VA* | | | *Miles from New River, VA* | |
| Outdoor Club at Virginia Tech | VA Sect. 33 | 210.8 | Peters Mountain (3,860') | | 16.5 | Central VA Map 4 |
| | | 213.0 | Dickenson Gap | | 14.3 | |
| | | 214.6 | Groundhog Trail | | 12.7 | |
| | | 215.6 | Symms Gap Meadow | | 11.7 | |
| | | 219.1 | Campsite, spring | Cw | 8.2 | |
| | | 220.6 | Rice Field Shelter (3,400') | S(nw) | 6.7 | |
| | | 221.2 | Spring | w | 6.1 | |
| | | 222.2 | Stream | w | 5.1 | |
| | | 223.4 | Clendennin Road (VA-641) | R | 3.9 | |
| | | 223.9 | Hemlock Ridge | | 3.4 | |
| | | 227.3 | US-460, Senator Shumate Bridge (east end), New River (1,600') | R | 0.0 | |

# Southwest Virginia

| Club | GBS | NtoS | Features | Facilities (see page 14 for codes) | StoN | Map |
|---|---|---|---|---|---|---|
| | | *Miles from New River, VA* | | | *Miles from Damascus, VA* | |
| Roanoke A.T. Club | VA Section 34 | 0.0 | US-460, Senator Shumate Bridge (east end), New River (1,600') | R | 166.8 | SW VA Map 1 |
| | | 0.4 | VA 100, **Pearisburg, VA, P.O. 24134** (P.O.,G,L,M 1.3m E) | ★ RGLM | 166.4 | |
| | | 1.4 | VA-634 | R | 165.4 | |
| | | 3.4 | Angels Rest, Pearis Mountain (3,550') | | 163.4 | |
| | | 3.9 | Campsite, spring | Cw | 162.9 | |
| | | 9.8 | Doc's Knob Shelter | Sw | 157.0 | |
| | | 12.1 | Sugar Run Gap, Sugar Run Gap Rd. (VA 663) (L 0.5m E) | RL | 154.7 | |
| | | 13.7 | Big Horse Gap, USFS-103 (3,752') | R | 153.1 | |
| | | 13.8 | Ribble Trail, north junction | w | 153.0 | |
| | | 19.3 | Wapiti Shelter (2,600') | Sw | 147.5 | |
| | | 21.1 | Stream | w | 145.7 | |
| | | 21.4 | Ribble Trail, south junction | | 145.4 | |
| | | 23.5 | Walnut Flats Campground (C,w 0.4m W) | Cw | 143.3 | |
| | | 25.4 | Dismal Creek Falls Trail | | 141.4 | |
| | VA Section 35 | 27.3 | VA-606 (2,040') (C,G,M,w 0.5m W; L,M 0.5m E) | RCGLMw | 139.5 | |
| | | 27.4 | Kimberling Creek | | 139.4 | |
| | | 29.2 | Brushy Mountain (2,800') | | 137.6 | |
| | VA Section 36 | 32.6 | VA-608, Lickskillet Hollow (2,200') | R | 134.2 | |
| | | 33.8 | Jenny Knob Shelter | Sw | 133.0 | |
| | | 35.5 | Brushy Mountain (3,101') | | 131.3 | |
| OC at VA Tech | | 36.9 | VA-611 | R | 129.9 | SW VA Map 2 |
| | | 43.5 | Helveys Mill Shelter (S,w 0.3m E) | Sw | 123.3 | |
| | | 44.9 | VA-612, Kimberling Creek | R | 121.9 | |
| | | 45.3 | I-77 Crossing | R | 121.5 | |

# Southwest Virginia

| Club | GBS | NtoS | Features | Facilities (see page 14 for codes) | StoN | Map |
|---|---|---|---|---|---|---|
| | | *Miles from New River, VA* | | | *Miles from Damascus, VA* | |
| Piedmont A.T. Hikers | | 45.7 | US-52 (2,920'); **Bastian, VA, P.O. 24314; Bland, VA, P.O. 24315** (P.O. 1.8m W; P.O.,G,L,M 2.7m E) | ★ RGLM | 121.1 | SW VA Map 2 |
| | VA Section 37 | 50.5 | Trail Boss Trail | | 116.3 | |
| | | 52.6 | VA-615, Laurel Creek (2,450') | RCw | 114.2 | |
| | | 53.4 | Brushy Mountain (3,080') | | 113.4 | |
| | | 57.0 | Jenkins Shelter (2,470') | Sw | 109.8 | |
| | | 57.9 | Stream | w | 108.9 | |
| | | 60.5 | Davis Farm Campsite (C,w 0.4m W) | Cw | 106.3 | |
| | VA Section 38 | 61.5 | VA-623, Garden Mountain (3,880') | R | 105.3 | |
| | | 66.3 | Walker Gap (3,520') (w 0.2m E) | Rw | 100.5 | |
| | | 67.7 | Chestnut Knob Shelter (4,409') | S(nw) | 99.1 | |
| | | 69.5 | Spring-fed pond | w | 97.3 | |
| | | 72.3 | USFS-222 (2,300') | R | 94.5 | |
| | | 73.7 | Lick Creek (ford) | w | 93.1 | |
| | | 76.0 | Lynn Camp Creek (2,400') | w | 90.8 | |
| | | 76.6 | Campsite, stream | Cw | 90.2 | |
| | | 77.1 | Knot Maul Branch Shelter | S | 89.7 | |
| | | 78.3 | Brushy Mountain (3,200') | | 88.5 | |
| | VA Section 39 | 79.2 | VA-42; Ceres, VA, P.O. 24318 | R | 87.6 | |
| | | 79.8 | Spring | w | 87.0 | |
| | | 80.2 | VA-742, North Fork of Holston River | | 86.6 | |
| | | 81.7 | VA-610 | R | 85.1 | |
| | | 83.2 | Tilson Gap, Big Walker Mountain (3,500') | | 83.6 | SW VA 3 |
| | | 85.1 | Crawfish Valley (2,600') | Cw | 81.7 | |
| | | 86.2 | Little Brushy Mountain (3,300') | | 80.6 | |

# Southwest Virginia

| Club | GBS | NtoS | Features | Facilities (see page 14 for codes) | StoN | Map |
|---|---|---|---|---|---|---|
| | | *Miles from New River, VA* | | | *Miles from Damascus, VA* | |
| Piedmont A.T. Hikers | VA Sect. 39 | 89.0 | Davis Path Campsite | C(nw) | 77.8 | SW VA Map 3 |
| | | 90.1 | Spring | w | 76.7 | |
| | | 90.8 | VA-617 | R | 76.0 | |
| | VA Section 40 | 91.8 | VA-683, US-11, I-81 (2,420');<br>**Atkins, VA, P.O. 24311**<br>(P.O. 3.1m W; G,L,M on A.T.) | RGLM | 75.0 | |
| | | 94.1 | VA-729 | R | 72.7 | |
| | | 94.6 | VA-615 | R | 72.2 | |
| | | 96.1 | USFS-644 | R | 70.7 | |
| | | 96.4 | Chatfield Shelter | Sw | 70.4 | |
| | | 97.9 | Glade Mountain (4,093') | | 68.9 | |
| | | 99.2 | USFS-86 | Cw | 67.6 | |
| | | 99.6 | Locust Mountain | | 67.2 | |
| | | 100.6 | Brushy Mountain | | 66.2 | |
| | | 102.5 | VA-622 | R | 64.3 | |
| | VA Section 41 | 103.2 | VA-16 (3,220');<br>**Sugar Grove, VA, P.O. 24375**<br>**Marion, VA, P.O. 24354**<br>(P.O.,G 3.1m E; P.O., G,L,M 6.6m W) | ★<br>RGLMw | 63.6 | |
| | | 103.4 | Partnership Shelter | Sw | 63.4 | |
| | | 107.3 | VA-601 | R | 59.5 | |
| Mt. Rogers A.T. Club | | 111.1 | VA-670 (Teas Road),<br>South Fork Holston River (2,450') | R | 55.7 | |
| | | 112.0 | VA-672 | R | 54.8 | |
| | | 113.2 | Trimpi Shelter | Sw | 53.6 | |
| | | 115.3 | High Point (4,040') | | 51.5 | |
| | | 115.8 | Bobby's Trail, Raccoon Branch Campground<br>(C,w 0.2m E; 3.3m E) | Cw | 51.0 | |

# Southwest Virginia

| Club | GBS | NtoS | Features | Facilities (see page 14 for codes) | StoN | Map |
|---|---|---|---|---|---|---|
| | | *Miles from New River, VA* | | | *Miles from Damascus, VA* | |
| Mt. Rogers A.T. Club | VA Section 42 | 117.3 | Dickey Gap, VA-16, VA-650; **Troutdale, VA, P.O. 24378** (P.O. 2.7m E; L 2.3m E) | RL | 49.5 | SW VA Map 3 |
| | | 118.5 | Comers Creek, Comers Creek Falls Trail (3,200') | w | 48.3 | |
| | | 118.9 | Dickey Gap Trail | Cw | 47.9 | |
| | | 121.0 | Stream | w | 45.8 | |
| | | 121.8 | Hurricane Creek Trail | | 45.0 | |
| | | 122.4 | Hurricane Mountain Shelter | Sw | 44.4 | |
| | | 123.3 | Chestnut Flats, Iron Mountain Trail | | 43.5 | |
| | | 123.6 | Hurricane Mountain (4,320'), Tennessee-New River Divide | | 43.2 | |
| | VA Section 43 | 125.6 | VA-603, Fox Creek (3,480') | Rw | 41.2 | |
| | | 127.3 | Old Orchard Shelter | Sw | 39.5 | |
| | | 128.9 | Pine Mountain Trail (5,000') | | 37.9 | |
| | | 130.3 | The Scales | | 36.5 | SW VA Map 4 |
| | | 130.7 | Stone Mountain | | 36.1 | |
| | | 133.0 | Wilson Creek Trail (Cw 1.3m E) | Cw | 33.8 | |
| | | 133.2 | Big Wilson Creek | Cw | 33.6 | |
| | | 133.3 | Grayson Highlands State Park, Wise Shelter (4,460') | Sw | 33.5 | |
| | | 135.4 | Park service road to Massie Gap | | 31.4 | |
| | | 136.2 | Wilburn Ridge | | 30.6 | |
| | | 137.4 | Rhododendron Gap (5,440') | | 29.4 | |
| | | 138.4 | Thomas Knob Shelter | Sw | 28.4 | |
| | | 138.6 | Mt. Rogers Spur Trail | | 28.2 | |
| | | 140.6 | Deep Gap (w 0.2m E) | w | 26.2 | |
| | | 142.6 | VA-600, Elk Garden (4,434') | R | 24.2 | |
| | | 145.0 | Whitetop Mountain Road (USFS-89) | R | 21.8 | |

# Southwest Virginia

| Club | GBS | NtoS | Features | Facilities (see page 14 for codes) | StoN | Map |
|---|---|---|---|---|---|---|
| | | *Miles from New River, VA* | | | *Miles from Damascus, VA* | |
| Mt. Rogers A.T. Club | VA Section 44 | 145.1 | Spring | w | 21.7 | SW VA Map 4 |
| | | 145.9 | Buzzard Rock (5,080'), Whitetop Mountain | | 20.9 | |
| | | 148.4 | VA-601 (Beech Mountain Road) | Rw | 18.4 | |
| | | 149.7 | US-58 (3,160'); Summit Cut, VA | R | 17.1 | |
| | VA Section 45 | 150.8 | Lost Mountain Shelter | Sw | 16.0 | |
| | | 152.0 | VA-859 (Grassy Ridge Road) | R | 14.8 | |
| | | 152.6 | Virginia Creeper Trail, Whitetop Laurel Creek | | 14.2 | |
| | | 153.2 | VA-728, Creek Junction (2,720') (R 0.5m E) | R | 13.6 | |
| | | 155.0 | Bear Tree Gap side trail (C 0.6m W) | C | 11.8 | |
| | | 157.3 | Saunders Shelter (S,w 0.2m W) | Sw | 9.5 | |
| | | 157.6 | Straight Mountain (3,500') | | 9.2 | |
| | | 159.2 | Taylors Valley Side Trail (M 0.6m E) | M | 7.6 | |
| | | 159.8 | Stream | w | 7.0 | |
| | | 161.2 | US-58, Straight Branch, Feathercamp Branch (2,200'), Feathercamp Trail | Rw | 5.6 | |
| | | 161.8 | Beech Grove Trail | | 5.0 | |
| | | 163.3 | Feathercamp Ridge, Iron Mountain Trail (2,850') | | 3.5 | |
| | | 165.8 | US-58, VA-91, Virginia Creeper Trail | R | 1.0 | |
| | | 166.8 | **Damascus, VA, P.O. 24236 (1,928')** (P.O.,G,L,M on A.T.) | ★ RGLM | 0.0 | |

# Tennessee–North Carolina

| Club | GBS | N to S | Features | Facilities (see page 14 for codes) | S to N | Map |
|---|---|---|---|---|---|---|
| | | *Miles from Damascus, VA* | | | *Miles from Fontana Dam, NC* | |
| MRATC | TN-NC Section 1 | 0.0 | **Damascus, VA, P.O. 24236** (1,928') (P.O.,G,L,M on A.T.) | ★ RGLM | 304.0 | TN-NC Map 1 |
| | | 2.1 | Campsite | Cw | 301.9 | |
| | | 3.7 | Virginia–Tennessee Line | | 300.3 | |
| Tennessee Eastman Hiking Club | | 4.8 | Backbone Rock Trail | | 299.2 | |
| | | 10.2 | Abingdon Gap Shelter (3,785') | CSw | 293.8 | |
| | | 11.3 | McQueens Gap, USFS-69 | R | 292.7 | |
| | | 11.7 | McQueens Knob | | 292.3 | |
| | | 13.1 | Double Spring Gap | Cw | 290.9 | |
| | TN-NC Section 2 | 15.0 | Low Gap, US-421 (3,384'); **Shady Valley, TN, P.O. 37688** (w on A.T.; P.O.,G,M 3m E) | RGMw | 289.0 | |
| | | 18.5 | Double Springs Shelter, Holston Mountain Trail (4,080') | CSw | 285.5 | |
| | | 19.4 | Campsite (north of Osborne Farm) | Cw | 284.6 | |
| | TN-NC Section 3 | 21.5 | TN-91 (3,450') | R | 282.5 | |
| | | 22.4 | Stream | w | 281.6 | |
| | | 24.8 | Spring | w | 279.2 | |
| | | 24.9 | Nick Grindstaff Monument | | 279.1 | |
| | | 26.2 | Iron Mountain Shelter (4,125') | CS(nw) | 277.8 | |
| | | 26.4 | Spring | w | 277.6 | |
| | | 27.8 | Turkeypen Gap | | 276.2 | |
| | | 28.2 | Big Laurel Branch Wilderness (north end) | | 275.8 | |
| | | 29.2 | Campsite at boggy spring | Cw | 274.8 | |
| | | 33.0 | Vandeventer Shelter (3,510') (C,S on A.T.; w 0.5m W) | CSw | 271.0 | |
| | | 34.7 | Spring | w | 269.3 | |
| | | 37.7 | Wilbur Dam Road | R | 266.3 | |
| | | 39.0 | Watauga Dam (north end) | | 265.0 | |
| | | 40.2 | Stream (2,100') | w | 263.8 | |

# Tennessee–North Carolina

| Club | GBS | N to S (Miles from Damascus, VA) | Features | Facilities (see page 14 for codes) | S to N (Miles from Fontana Dam, NC) | Map |
|---|---|---|---|---|---|---|
| Tennessee Eastman Hiking Club | TN-NC Section 4 | 40.6 | Griffith Branch | w | 263.4 | TN-NC Map 1 |
| | | 42.1 | US-321; **Hampton, TN, P.O. 37658** (P.O.,G,M 2.6m W; G,L 1.8m W) | RGLM | 261.9 | |
| | | 42.6 | Campsite south of Pond Mtn. Wilderness | C(nw) | 261.4 | |
| | | 45.2 | Pond Flats | Cw | 258.8 | |
| | | 48.0 | Hampton Blueline Trail to US-321 | w | 256.0 | |
| | | 48.5 | Waycaster Spring | w | 255.5 | |
| | | 49.5 | Laurel Fork Falls | w | 254.5 | |
| | TN-NC Section 5 | 50.7 | Dennis Cove, USFS-50 (C,G,L,M 0.5m E; C,L 0.2m W) | RCGLMw | 253.3 | |
| | | 52.4 | Side trail to Coon Den Falls | | 251.6 | TN-NC Map 2 |
| | | 54.9 | Canute Place | Cw | 249.1 | |
| | | 55.8 | Tower Road, White Rocks Mountain (4,206') | R | 248.2 | |
| | | 57.0 | Moreland Gap | Cw | 247.0 | |
| | | 60.1 | Hardcore Cascades | w | 243.9 | |
| | | 62.8 | Laurel Fork | w | 241.2 | |
| | | 63.8 | Stream | w | 240.2 | |
| | | 65.0 | Walnut Mountain Road | R | 239.0 | |
| | | 65.8 | Campsite south of Slide Hollow | Cw | 238.2 | |
| | | 66.6 | Mountaineer Falls Shelter | Sw | 237.4 | |
| | | 66.8 | Mountaineer Falls Campsite | Cw | 237.2 | |
| | | 71.8 | Campbell Hollow Road | R | 232.2 | |
| | | 72.1 | Buck Mountain Road | R | 231.9 | |
| | | 75.2 | Bear Branch Road | R | 228.8 | |
| | | 75.4 | US-19E (2,895'); **Roan Mountain, TN, P.O. 37687** (P.O.,G,M 3.4m W) | ★ RCGLM | 228.6 | |
| | | | **Elk Park, NC, P.O. 28622;** (P.O. 2.5m E; C 4.0m E; G 1.2m E; L 3m E; M 0.5m E, 1m E) | RCGLM | 228.6 | |

# Tennessee–North Carolina

| Club | GBS | NtoS | Features | Facilities (see page 14 for codes) | StoN | Map |
|---|---|---|---|---|---|---|
| | | *Miles from Damascus, VA* | | | *Miles from Fontana Dam, NC* | |
| Tennessee Eastman Hiking Club | | 76.0 | Apple House Campsite | Cw | 228.0 | TN-NC Map 2 |
| | | 76.1 | Wilder Mine Hollow Group Campsite | Cw | 227.9 | |
| | | 78.4 | Doll Flats | Cw | 225.6 | |
| | TN-NC Section 6 | 80.8 | Hump Mountain (5,587') | | 223.2 | |
| | | 81.7 | Bradley Gap | Cw | 222.3 | |
| | | 83.0 | Little Hump Mountain (5,459') | Cw | 221.0 | |
| | | 84.6 | Yellow Mountain Gap (4,682') (w 0.2m E; C 0.3m E) | Cw | 219.4 | |
| | | 86.5 | Stan Murray Shelter (5,050') | CSw | 217.5 | |
| | | 88.3 | Side trail to Grassy Ridge | | 215.7 | |
| | Section 7 | 90.2 | Carvers Gap, TN-143, NC-261 (5,512') | Rw | 213.8 | |
| | | 93.8 | Ash Gap | Cw | 210.2 | |
| | TN-NC Section 8 | 96.8 | Hughes Gap (4,040') (G 3.2m W; C,L 2m E) | RCGL | 207.2 | |
| | | 99.0 | Little Rock Knob (4,918') | C(nw) | 205.0 | |
| | | 100.2 | Clyde Smith Shelter | CSw | 203.8 | |
| | | 101.3 | Campsite at row of maple trees | Cw | 202.7 | |
| | | 102.1 | Greasy Creek Gap (4,034') (C,w 0.2m W; L 0.7m E) | CLw | 201.9 | |
| | | 105.0 | Orchard Campsite | Cw | 199.0 | |
| | | | The A.T. has been closed from just south of the Orchard Campsite (mile 105.0) to Low Gap (mile 110.4) due to damage from Hurricane Helene in September 2024. It will likely reopen in Spring 2026, but until then, a detour has been established. For more information, visit appalachiantrail.org/IronMtnGap. | | | |
| | TN-NC Section 9 | 106.2 | Iron Mountain Gap, TN-107, NC-226 (3,723') (G 4.7m W) | RG | 197.8 | |
| | | 110.4 | Low Gap (3,900') | w | 193.6 | |
| | | 112.6 | Unaka Mountain (5,180') | | 191.4 | |
| | | 113.6 | USFS-230 | R | 190.4 | |

# Tennessee–North Carolina

Club | GBS | NtoS | Features | Facilities (see page 14 for codes) | StoN | Map

| Miles from Damascus, VA | Features | Facilities | Miles from Fontana Dam, NC |
|---|---|---|---|
| 114.2 | Beauty Spot Gap (4,100') | RCw | 189.8 |
| 115.5 | Spring | Rw | 188.5 |
| 115.8 | Beauty Spot | RC(nw) | 188.2 |
| 117.0 | USFS-230 | R | 187.0 |
| 118.1 | Indian Grave Gap, TN-395 (C 3.3m W) | RC | 185.9 |
| 120.9 | Spring | w | 183.1 |
| 122.2 | Curley Maple Gap Shelter (3,070') | CSw | 181.8 |
| 125.1 | Nolichucky River Valley | | 178.9 |
| 126.4 | Nolichucky River (1,700'); **Erwin, TN, P.O. 37650** ★ (P.O.,G,M 3.8m W; L 1.2m W; G,L 2.3m W) | RGLM | 177.6 |

The Chestoa Bridge that carried the A.T. over the Nolichucky River was swept away during Hurricane Helene in September 2024. During peak thru-hiking season (April to mid-June), a free ferry is provided by ATC. At other times, hikers must use a 3.6-mile roadwalk detour. For more information, visit appalachiantrail.org/NolichuckyRiver.

| Miles from Damascus, VA | Features | Facilities | Miles from Fontana Dam, NC |
|---|---|---|---|
| 130.3 | Temple Hill Gap (2,850') | | 173.7 |
| 132.7 | No Business Knob Shelter | CSw | 171.3 |
| 132.9 | Spring | w | 171.1 |
| 135.3 | Devils Creek Gap (3,400') | R | 168.7 |
| 137.0 | Oglesby Branch | w | 167.0 |
| 137.6 | Spivey Gap, US-19W (3,200') | Rw | 166.4 |
| 138.1 | Campsite | Cw | 165.9 |
| 139.6 | Trail to High Rocks (4,100') | | 164.4 |
| 139.9 | Whistling Gap | Cw | 164.1 |
| 141.9 | Little Bald | | 162.1 |
| 142.9 | Campsite | Cw | 161.1 |
| 143.3 | Bald Mountain Shelter | Sw | 160.7 |
| 144.2 | Big Stamp | | |

Tennessee Eastman Hiking Club · Carolina Mountain Club
TN-NC Section 9 · TN-NC Section 10 · TN-NC Section 11
TN-NC Map 2 · TN-NC Map 3

# Tennessee–North Carolina

| Club | GBS | NtoS | Features | Facilities (see page 14 for codes) | StoN | Map |
|---|---|---|---|---|---|---|
| | | *Miles from Damascus, VA* | | | *Miles from Fontana Dam, NC* | |
| Carolina Mountain Club | TN-NC Section 11 | | (C,w 0.3m W; M 1.5m E) | CMw | 159.8 | TN-NC Map 3 |
| | | 144.5 | Big Bald (5,516') | | 159.5 | |
| | | 145.3 | Spring | w | 158.7 | |
| | | 147.3 | Low Gap | w | 156.7 | |
| | | 148.7 | Street Gap (4,100') | | 155.3 | |
| | | 150.3 | Springs | w | 153.7 | |
| | TN-NC Section 12 | 151.0 | Sams Gap, US-23, I-26 (3,800') | | | |
| | | | (M 1.9m E, 2.8m E; G 3.2m E) | RGM | 153.0 | |
| | | 152.8 | High Rock (4,460') | | 151.2 | |
| | | 153.4 | Hogback Ridge Shelter | | | |
| | | | (C,S 0.1m E; w 0.3m E) | CSw | 150.6 | |
| | | 154.6 | Rice Gap (3,800') | | 149.4 | |
| | | 155.6 | Big Flat | C | 148.4 | |
| | | 156.2 | Frozen Knob (4,579') | | 147.8 | |
| | | 159.0 | Rector Laurel Road (2,960') | R | 145.0 | |
| | TN-NC Section 13 | 159.5 | Devil Fork Gap, NC-212 | R | 144.5 | |
| | | 161.3 | Campsite | Cw | 142.7 | |
| | | 162.2 | Flint Mountain Shelter (3,550') | CSw | 141.8 | |
| | | 163.8 | Spring | w | 140.2 | |
| | | 167.0 | Big Butt (4,750') | C | 137.0 | |
| | | 168.9 | Jerry Cabin Shelter (4,150') | CSw | 135.1 | |
| | | 171.4 | Big Firescald Knob | w | 132.6 | |
| | | 172.4 | Blackstack Cliffs (0.1m W) | | 131.6 | |
| | | 172.6 | White Rock Cliffs (0.1m E | | 131.4 | |
| | | 172.7 | Spring | w | 131.3 | |
| | | 174.4 | Camp Creek Bald, | | | |
| | | | side trail to fire tower (4,750') | R | 129.6 | |
| | | 176.2 | Little Laurel Shelter (3,300') | CSw | 127.8 | |
| | | 181.1 | Allen Gap, NC-208, TN-70 (2,234') | Rw | 122.9 | |
| | | 183.3 | Spring | w | 120.7 | |

# Tennessee–North Carolina

| Club | GBS | NtoS Miles from Damascus, VA | Features | Facilities (see page 14 for codes) | StoN Miles from Fontana Dam, NC | Map |
|---|---|---|---|---|---|---|
| Carolina Mountain Club | TN-NC Section 14 | 184.8 | Spring Mountain Shelter (3,300') | CSw | 119.2 | TN-NC Map 4 |
| | | 186.5 | Hurricane Gap | R | 117.5 | |
| | | 187.6 | Rich Mountain Fire Tower Side Trail (3,600') | Cw | 116.4 | |
| | | 189.9 | Tanyard Gap, US-25 & US-70 (2,278') | R | 114.1 | |
| | | 192.5 | Pump Gap | | 111.5 | |
| | | 194.4 | Lovers Leap Rock | | 109.6 | |
| | TN-NC Section 15 | 195.8 | US-25 & US-70, NC-209 (1,326'); **Hot Springs, NC, P.O. 28743** (P.O.,C,G,L,M on A.T.) | ★ RCGLM | 108.2 | |
| | | 199.0 | Deer Park Mountain Shelter | CSw | 105.0 | |
| | | 202.4 | Garenflo Gap (2,500') | R | 101.6 | |
| | | 204.9 | Big Rock Spring | w | 99.1 | |
| | | 206.5 | Bluff Mountain (4,686') | | 97.5 | |
| | | 208.9 | Campsite (C 0.1m W) | Cw | 95.1 | |
| | | 210.2 | Lemon Gap, NC-1182, TN-107 (3,550') | R | 93.8 | |
| | | 213.7 | Roaring Fork Shelter | CSw | 90.3 | |
| | | 215.6 | Max Patch Summit (4,629') | | 88.4 | |
| | TN-NC Section 16 | 216.4 | Max Patch Road (NC-1182) | R | 87.6 | |
| | | 219.1 | Brown Gap | Rw | 84.9 | |
| | | 222.0 | Deep Gap, Groundhog Creek Shelter (2,900') (C,S,w 0.2m E) | CSw | 82.0 | |
| | | 224.0 | Campsite | Cw | 80.0 | |
| | | 224.5 | Snowbird Mountain (4,263') | R | 79.5 | |
| | | 226.0 | Spanish Oak Gap | | 78.0 | |
| | | 226.9 | Painter Branch | Cw | 77.1 | |
| | | 229.2 | Green Corner Road (C,G,L 0.2m W) | RCGL | 74.8 | |

# Tennessee–North Carolina

| Club | GBS | NtoS<br>Miles from Damascus, VA | Features | Facilities (see page 14 for codes) | StoN<br>Miles from Fontana Dam, NC | Map |
|---|---|---|---|---|---|---|
| CMC | Section 16 | 229.7 | I-40 | R | 74.3 | Map 4 |
| | | 230.1 | Pigeon River (1,400') | | 73.9 | |
| | | 230.3 | State Line Branch | Cw | 73.7 | |
| Smoky Mountains Hiking Club | TN-NC Section 17 (NC 1) | 231.6 | Davenport Gap, TN-32, NC-1397; eastern boundary, Great Smoky Mountains National Park (1,975') (C 2.5m E) | RC | 72.4 | Great Smoky Mtns. N.P. Map |
| | | 232.7 | Davenport Gap Shelter | Sw | 71.3 | |
| | | 234.9 | Spring | w | 69.1 | |
| | | 236.4 | Spring | w | 67.6 | |
| | | 236.8 | Mt. Cammerer Side Trail (5,000') | | 67.2 | |
| | | 238.9 | Low Gap Trail | | 65.1 | |
| | | 239.6 | Cosby Knob Shelter | Sw | 64.4 | |
| | | 240.0 | Cosby Knob | | 64.0 | |
| | | 243.3 | Snake Den Ridge Trail | | 60.7 | |
| | | 245.3 | Guyot Spring | w | 58.7 | |
| | | 245.9 | Guyot Spur (6,360') | | 58.1 | |
| | | 247.3 | Tri-Corner Knob Shelter, Balsam Mtn. Trail | Sw | 56.7 | |
| | | 248.4 | Mt. Chapman | | 55.6 | |
| | | 250.1 | Mt. Sequoyah | | 53.9 | |
| | | 252.5 | Hughes Ridge Trail to Pecks Corner Shelter (w on A.T.; S,w 0.5m E) | Sw | 51.5 | |
| | | 254.5 | Bradleys View | | 49.5 | |
| | | 257.6 | Porters Gap, The Sawteeth | | 46.4 | |
| | | 259.0 | Charlies Bunion | | 45.0 | |
| | | 259.9 | Icewater Spring Shelter | Sw | 44.1 | |
| | | 260.2 | Boulevard Trail to Mt. LeConte | | 43.8 | |
| | | 263.0 | Newfound Gap, US 441 (5,045') | Rw | 41.0 | |
| | | 264.7 | Indian Gap, Road Prong Trail | R | 39.3 | |
| | | 266.1 | Spring | w | 37.9 | |

# Tennessee–North Carolina

| Club | GBS | NtoS | Features | Facilities (see page 14 for codes) | StoN | Map |
|---|---|---|---|---|---|---|
| | | *Miles from Damascus, VA* | | | *Miles from Fontana Dam, NC* | |
| Smoky Mountains Hiking Club | TN-NC Section 18 (NC 2) | 267.9 | Sugarland Mtn. Trail to Mt. Collins Shelter (5,900') (S,w 0.5m W) | Sw | 36.1 | Great Smoky Mtns. N.P. Map |
| | | 270.2 | Mt. Love | | 33.8 | |
| | | 270.7 | Kuwohi (Clingmans Dome) (6,643') (R,w 0.5m E) | Rw | 33.3 | |
| | | 273.5 | Double Spring Gap Shelter (5,507') | Sw | 30.5 | |
| | | 275.0 | Silers Bald | | 29.0 | |
| | | 275.2 | Silers Bald Shelter | Sw | 28.8 | |
| | | 278.2 | Buckeye Gap (4,817'), Miry Ridge Trail | w | 25.8 | |
| | | 280.6 | Sams Gap, Greenbrier Ridge Trail | w | 23.4 | |
| | | 280.9 | Derrick Knob Shelter | Sw | 23.1 | |
| | | 281.9 | Sugar Tree Gap (4,435') | | 22.1 | |
| | | 283.6 | Mineral Gap (5,030') | | 20.4 | |
| | | 284.2 | Beechnut Gap | w | 19.8 | |
| | | 285.3 | Thunderhead, east peak (5,527') | | 18.7 | |
| | | 285.9 | Rocky Top | | 18.1 | |
| | | 287.0 | Eagle Creek Trail to Spence Field Shelter, Bote Mountain Trail (S,w 0.2m E) | Sw | 17.0 | |
| | | 289.9 | Russell Field Shelter | Sw | 14.1 | |
| | | 291.4 | Little Abrams Gap (4,120') | | 12.6 | |
| | | 292.5 | Devils Tater Patch (4,775') | | 11.5 | |
| | | 293.0 | Mollies Ridge Shelter | Sw | 11.0 | |
| | | 294.7 | Ekaneetlee Gap (3,842') | w | 9.3 | |
| | | 296.2 | Doe Knob (4,520'), Gregory Bald Trail | | 7.8 | |
| | | 298.4 | Birch Spring Gap; Campsite #113 | Cw | 5.6 | |
| | | 299.7 | Shuckstack fire tower (0.1m E) | | 4.3 | |
| | | 304.0 | Little Tennessee River, Fontana Dam; southern boundary, Great Smoky Mountains National Park (1,800') | R | 0.0 | |

# North Carolina–Georgia

| Club | GBS | NtoS Miles from Fontana Dam, NC | Features | Facilities (see page 14 for codes) | StoN Miles from Springer Mountain, GA | Map |
|---|---|---|---|---|---|---|
| Smoky Mountains Hiking Club | NC Section 3 | 0.0 | Little Tennessee River, Fontana Dam; southern boundary, Great Smoky Mountains National Park (1,740') | R | 167.0 | NC-GA Map 1 |
| | | 0.4 | Fontana Dam Visitor Center | Rw | 166.6 | |
| | | 0.8 | "Fontana Hilton" Shelter | CSw | 166.2 | |
| | | 2.1 | NC-28; Fontana Marina **Fontana Dam, NC, P.O. 28733** (P.O.,G,L,M 1.8m W) | ★ RGLM | 164.9 | |
| | | 4.4 | Campsite | Cw | 162.6 | |
| | | 4.8 | Walker Gap (3,450') | | 162.2 | |
| | | 6.2 | Black Gum Gap | | 160.8 | |
| | | 7.6 | Cable Gap Shelter | CSw | 159.4 | |
| | NC Section 4 | 8.5 | Yellow Creek Gap, NC-1242 (2,980') (Yellow Creek Mountain Road) (L 4m E) | RL | 158.5 | |
| | | 10.9 | Cody Gap | Cw | 156.1 | |
| | | 11.7 | Hogback Gap | | 155.3 | |
| | | 13.5 | Brown Fork Gap | w | 153.5 | |
| | | 13.9 | Brown Fork Gap Shelter | Sw | 153.1 | |
| | | 15.3 | Sweetwater Gap | | 151.7 | |
| | NC Section 5 | 16.3 | Stecoah Gap, NC-143 (3,165') (Sweetwater Creek Road) | R | 150.7 | |
| | | 18.4 | Simp Gap | | 148.6 | |
| | | 19.4 | Locust Cove Gap | Cw | 147.6 | |
| | | 21.8 | Cheoah Bald (5,062') | | 145.2 | |
| | | 23.0 | Sassafras Gap Shelter | CSw | 144.0 | |
| | | 23.9 | Swim Bald | | 143.1 | |
| | | 27.0 | Grassy Gap (3,050') | | 140.0 | |
| | | 28.5 | Wright Gap | R | 138.5 | |

# North Carolina–Georgia

| Club | GBS | NtoS | Features | Facilities (see page 14 for codes) | StoN | Map |
|---|---|---|---|---|---|---|
| | | *Miles from Fontana Dam, NC* | | | *Miles from Springer Mountain, GA* | |
| Nantahala Hiking Club | NC Section 6 | 30.1 | US-19, US-74, Nantahala River (1,723'); Wesser, NC (L,M on A.T.; G 1m E) | RGLM | 136.9 | NC-GA Map 2 |
| | | 30.9 | A. Rufus Morgan Shelter | CSw | 136.1 | |
| | | 34.0 | Jump-up Lookout (4,000') | | 133.0 | |
| | | 35.8 | Wesser Creek Trail, Wesser Bald Shelter | CS | 131.2 | |
| | | 35.9 | Spring | w | 131.1 | |
| | | 36.6 | Wesser Bald (4,627'), viewing tower (0.1m E) | | 130.4 | |
| | NC Section 7 | 38.0 | Tellico Gap, NC-1365 (3,850') | R | 129.0 | |
| | | 39.4 | Big Branch Campsite | Cw | 127.6 | |
| | | 39.7 | Side trail to Rocky Bald Lookout | | 127.3 | |
| | | 40.9 | Copper Ridge Bald Lookout (5,080') | | 126.1 | |
| | | 41.6 | Cold Spring Shelter | CSw | 125.4 | |
| | | 42.8 | Burningtown Gap, NC-1397 (4,236') | R | 124.2 | |
| | | 45.1 | Licklog Gap (C 0.1 W, w 0.3m W) | Cw | 121.9 | |
| | | 46.4 | Wayah Shelter | CSw | 120.6 | |
| | | 46.9 | Campsite | Cw | 120.1 | |
| | | 47.3 | Wayah Bald (5,342') | R | 119.7 | |
| | | 49.2 | Wine Spring | Cw | 117.8 | |
| | | 49.7 | USFS-69 | Rw | 117.3 | |
| | NC Section 8 | 51.5 | Wayah Gap, NC-1310 (4,180') | R | 115.5 | |
| | | 53.2 | Siler Bald Shelter (4,700') (C,S,w 0.5m E) | CSw | 113.8 | |
| | | 55.4 | Panther Gap | | 111.6 | |
| | | 56.3 | Swinging Lick Gap | | 110.7 | |
| | | 56.5 | Moore Creek Campsite | Cw | 110.5 | |
| | | 57.4 | Winding Stair Gap, US-64; **Franklin, NC, P.O. 28734** (w on A.T.; P.O.,G,L,M 10m E) | ★ RGLMw | 109.6 | |

# North Carolina–Georgia

| Club | GBS | NtoS | Features | Facilities (see page 14 for codes) | StoN | Map |
|---|---|---|---|---|---|---|
| | | *Miles from Fontana Dam, NC* | | | *Miles from Springer Mountain, GA* | |
| Nantahala Hiking Club | NC Section 9 | 60.5 | Wallace Gap, "Old 64" (3,738') | R | 106.5 | NC-GA Map 2 |
| | | 61.1 | Rock Gap, Standing Indian Campground (C 1.5m W) | RC | 105.9 | |
| | | 61.2 | Rock Gap Shelter | CSw | 105.8 | |
| | | 63.7 | Glassmine Gap | | 103.3 | |
| | | 64.6 | Long Branch Shelter | CSw | 102.4 | |
| | | 67.1 | Albert Mountain (5,250') | | 99.9 | |
| | | 67.4 | Bearpen Trail, USFS-67 | R | 99.6 | |
| | | 68.4 | Spring | w | 98.6 | |
| | | 68.7 | Mooney Gap, USFS-83 | R | 98.3 | |
| | | 69.6 | Betty Creek Gap (4,300') | Cw | 97.4 | |
| | | 73.3 | Carter Gap Shelter | CSw | 93.7 | |
| | | 73.7 | Timber Ridge Trail | | 93.3 | |
| | | 76.5 | Beech Gap (4,460') | Cw | 90.5 | |
| | | 79.4 | Lower Ridge Trail, Standing Indian Mountain (5,498') (w 0.2m W) | w | 87.6 | |
| | | 80.9 | Standing Indian Shelter | CSw | 86.1 | |
| | NC Section 10 | 81.8 | Deep Gap, USFS-71 (4,341') (C 0.1m W) | CRw | 85.2 | |
| | | 83.9 | Wateroak Gap | | 83.1 | |
| | | 84.8 | Chunky Gal Trail | | 82.2 | |
| | | 85.0 | Whiteoak Stamp | Cw | 82.0 | |
| | | 85.8 | Muskrat Creek Shelter (4,600') | CSw | 81.2 | |
| | | 86.7 | Sassafras Gap | | 80.3 | |
| | | 88.6 | Bly Gap (3,840') | Cw | 78.4 | |
| GA A.T. Club | GA Section 11 | 88.7 | North Carolina–Georgia Line | | 78.3 | NC-GA Map 3 |
| | | 90.6 | Rich Cove Gap | | 76.4 | |
| | | 90.8 | Spring | w | 76.2 | |
| | | 91.8 | Blue Ridge Gap (3,020') | | 75.2 | |
| | | 92.4 | As Knob | | 74.6 | |

# North Carolina–Georgia

| Club | GBS | NtoS | Features | Facilities (see page 14 for codes) | StoN | Map |
|---|---|---|---|---|---|---|
| | | *Miles from Fontana Dam, NC* | | | *Miles from Springer Mountain, GA* | |
| Georgia A.T. Club | GA Section 11 | 93.1 | Plumorchard Gap Shelter (C,S,w 0.2m E) | CSw | 73.9 | NC-GA Map 3 |
| | | 94.3 | Bull Gap (3,550') | | 72.7 | |
| | | 95.8 | Cowart Gap | | 71.2 | |
| | | 96.5 | Little Bald Knob Campsite | Cw | 70.5 | |
| | GA Section 12 | 97.6 | Dicks Creek Gap, US-76 (2,675'); **Hiawassee, GA, P.O. 30546** (w on A.T.; L 3.5m W; P.O.,G,L,M 11m W) | ★ RGLMw | 69.4 | |
| | | 98.2 | Streams | w | 68.8 | |
| | | 98.8 | Moreland Gap | | 68.2 | |
| | | 99.8 | Powell Mountain (3,850') | | 67.2 | |
| | | 100.0 | McClure Gap | C | 67.0 | |
| | | 101.2 | Deep Gap Shelter (3,550') (C,S,w 0.3m E) | CSw | 65.8 | |
| | | 102.0 | Kelly Knob (4,276') | | 65.0 | |
| | | 103.0 | Addis Gap (3,304') (C,w 0.5m E) | Cw | 64.0 | |
| | | 103.9 | Sassafras Gap | w | 63.1 | |
| | | 105.0 | Swag of the Blue Ridge | | 62.0 | |
| | | 108.6 | Tray Mountain Shelter (C,S 0.2m W; w 0.3m W) | CSw | 58.4 | |
| | | 109.1 | Tray Mountain (4,430') | | 57.9 | |
| | | 109.9 | Tray Gap, Tray Mountain Road (USFS-79/698) | R | 57.1 | |
| | | 110.6 | Cheese Factory Site | Cw | 56.4 | |
| | | 110.9 | Tray Mountain Road (USFS-79) | R | 56.1 | |
| | | 111.6 | Indian Grave Gap, USFS 283 (3,113') | R | 55.4 | |
| | | 112.9 | Rocky Mountain (4,017') | C | 54.1 | |
| | | 113.7 | Stream | w | 53.3 | |

# North Carolina–Georgia

| Club | GBS | NtoS | Features | Facilities (see page 14 for codes) | StoN | Map |
|---|---|---|---|---|---|---|
| | | *Miles from Fontana Dam, NC* | | | *Miles from Springer Mountain, GA* | |
| Georgia A.T. Club | GA Section 13 | 114.3 | Unicoi Gap, GA-75 (2,949');<br>**Helen, GA, P.O. 30545**<br>(P.O.,G,L,M 9m E; C,G,L,M 3.8m W) | ★<br>RCGLM | 52.7 | NC-GA Map 3 |
| | | 115.8 | Blue Mountain (4,025') | | 51.2 | |
| | | 116.7 | Blue Mountain Shelter | CSw | 50.3 | |
| | | 117.4 | Spring | w | 49.6 | |
| | | 117.6 | Spaniards Knob Campsite | C | 49.4 | |
| | | 118.3 | Red Clay Gap | | 48.7 | |
| | | 119.0 | Chattahoochee Gap (3,500') | w | 48.0 | |
| | | 120.2 | Cold Springs Gap | | 46.8 | |
| | | 122.6 | Poplar Stamp Gap | Cw | 44.4 | |
| | | 124.0 | Low Gap Shelter (3,050') | CSw | 43.0 | |
| | | 124.8 | Sheep Rock Top | | 42.2 | |
| | | 126.7 | Poor Mountain | | 40.3 | |
| | | 127.9 | White Oak Stamp | | 39.1 | |
| | | 128.8 | Hogpen Gap, GA-348 (3,450') | Rw | 38.2 | |
| | | 129.0 | Whitley Gap Shelter<br>(S 1.2m E; w 1.5m E) | Sw | 38.0 | |
| | GA Section 14 | 129.7 | Tesnatee Gap, GA-348 (3,138') | R | 37.3 | |
| | | 130.7 | Cowrock Mountain (3,842') | | 36.3 | |
| | | 131.5 | Baggs Creek Gap | Cw | 35.5 | |
| | | 132.0 | Wolf Laurel Top | | 35.0 | |
| | | 132.7 | Rock Spring Top | w | 34.3 | |
| | | 133.5 | Swaim Gap | | 33.5 | |
| | | 134.2 | Levelland Mountain (3,942') | | 32.8 | |
| | | 134.6 | Bull Gap | Cw | 32.4 | NC-GA Map 4 |
| | Sect 15 | 135.7 | Neel Gap, US-19/129 (3,125')<br>(G,L on A.T.; L 0.3m E;<br>C,G 3m W; C,L 3.5m W) | ★<br>RCGLw | 31.3 | |

# North Carolina–Georgia

| Club | GBS | NtoS | Features | Facilities (see page 14 for codes) | StoN | Map |
|---|---|---|---|---|---|---|
| | | *Miles from Fontana Dam, NC* | | | *Miles from Springer Mountain, GA* | |
| Georgia A.T. Club | GA Section 15 | 136.7 | Flatrock Gap, Trail to Byron Reece Memorial (w 0.2m W) | w | 30.3 | NC-GA Map 4 |
| | | 138.1 | Blood Mountain Shelter (4,461') | S(nw) | 28.9 | |
| | | 138.9 | Blood Mountain Campsites | Cw | 28.1 | |
| | | 139.0 | Slaughter Creek Trail | w | 28.0 | |
| | | 139.3 | Bird Gap (3,650'), Woods Hole Shelter (S,w 0.5m W) | CSw | 27.7 | |
| | | 140.7 | Jarrard Gap (3,250') (w 0.3m W; w 1m W, G,L 2m W) | GLw | 26.3 | |
| | | 141.3 | Burnett Field Mountain | | 25.7 | |
| | | 143.0 | Lance Creek Campsite | Cw | 24.0 | |
| | | 144.1 | Dan Gap | | 22.9 | |
| | | 145.1 | Big Cedar Mountain (3,737') | | 21.9 | |
| | GA Section 16 | 146.5 | Woody Gap, GA-60 (3,173'); **Suches, GA, P.O. 30572** (w 0.1m W; P.O.,C,G 2m W) | ★ RCGw | 20.5 | |
| | | 148.0 | Ramrock Mountain | | 19.0 | |
| | | 150.1 | Gooch Gap, USFS-42 (2,821') | Rw | 16.9 | |
| | | 151.3 | Gooch Mountain Shelter (C,S,w 0.1m W) | CSw | 15.7 | |
| | | 152.8 | Justus Creek (2,550') | Cw | 14.2 | |
| | | 154.8 | Cooper Gap, USFS-42/80 | R | 12.2 | |
| | | 156.5 | Horse Gap (2,673') | R | 10.5 | |
| | GA Section 17 | 158.4 | Hightower Gap, USFS-42/69 (2,854') | R | 8.6 | |
| | | 158.9 | Hawk Mountain Shelter (S 0.2m W; w 0.4m W) | Sw | 8.1 | |
| | | 159.6 | Hawk Mountain Campsite | Cw | 7.4 | |
| | | 160.8 | USFS-251 | R | 6.2 | |
| | | 161.8 | Side trail to Long Creek Falls, junction with Benton MacKaye and Duncan Ridge trails | | 5.2 | |

# North Carolina–Georgia

| Club | GBS | NtoS | Features | Facilities (see page 14 for codes) | StoN | Map |
|---|---|---|---|---|---|---|
| | | *Miles from Fontana Dam, NC* | | | *Miles from Springer Mountain, GA* | |
| Georgia A.T. Club | GA Section 17 | 162.7 | Three Forks, USFS-58 (2,530') | RCw | 4.3 | NC-GA Map 4 |
| | | 162.8 | Benton MacKaye Trail | | 4.2 | |
| | | 163.2 | Stover Creek | w | 3.8 | |
| | | 164.1 | Stover Creek | w | 2.9 | |
| | | 164.2 | Stover Creek Shelter (C,S,w 0.2m E) | CSw | 2.8 | |
| | | 165.1 | Benton MacKaye Trail | | 1.9 | |
| | | 166.0 | USFS-42 | R | 1.0 | |
| | | 166.7 | Southern terminus, Benton MacKaye Trail | | 0.3 | |
| | | 166.8 | Springer Mountain Shelter (C,S,w 0.2m E) | CSw | 0.2 | |
| | | 167.0 | Springer Mountain (3,782') | | 0.0 | |

# Amicalola Falls Approach Trail

| Club | GBS | NtoS | Features | Facilities (see page 14 for codes) | StoN | Map |
|---|---|---|---|---|---|---|
| | | *Miles from Springer Mountain, GA* | | | *Miles from Amicalola Falls State Park* | |
| Georgia A.T. Club | Approach Trail | 0.0 | Springer Mountain (3,782') | | 8.8 | NC-GA Map 4 |
| | | 1.5 | Black Gap Shelter (temporarily closed) | Cw | 7.3 | |
| | | 2.8 | Nimblewill Gap, USFS-28 (3,100') | R | 6.0 | |
| | | 3.4 | Side trail to Len Foote Hike Inn (L,M,w 1m E) | LMw | 5.4 | |
| | | 3.7 | Frosty Mountain Road (USFS-46) | R | 5.1 | |
| | | 4.0 | Frosty Mountain (3,382') | Cw | 4.8 | |
| | | 5.6 | High Shoals Road | R | 3.2 | |
| | | 7.3 | USFS-46 | R | 1.5 | |
| | | 7.4 | Side trail to Len Foote Hike Inn (L,M,w 5m E) | LMw | 1.4 | |
| | | 7.6 | Amicalola Lodge Road (L,M,w 0.2m E) | RLMw | 1.2 | |
| | | 8.8 | Visitor Center, Amicalola Falls State Park (1,700') | RCSw | 0.0 | |

# A.T. Clubs

| | |
|---|---|
| Maine A.T. Club | www.matc.org |
| Appalachian Mountain Club | www.outdoors.org |
| Randolph Mountain Club | www.randolphmountainclub.org |
| Dartmouth Outing Club | www.outdoors.dartmouth.edu |
| Green Mountain Club | www.greenmountainclub.org |
| AMC Western Massachusetts Chapter | www.amc-wma.org |
| AMC Connecticut Chapter | www.ct-amc.org |
| New York–New Jersey Trail Conference | www.nynjtc.org |
| Batona Hiking Club | www.batona.wildapricot.org |
| AMC Delaware Valley Chapter | www.amcdv.org |
| Keystone Trails Association | www.kta-hike.org |
| Blue Mountain Eagle Climbing Club | www.bmecc.org |
| Allentown Hiking Club | www.allentownhikingclub.org |
| Susquehanna A.T. Club | www.satc-hike.org |
| York Hiking Club | www.yorkhikingclub.com |
| Cumberland Valley A.T. Club | www.cvatclub.org |
| Mountain Club of Maryland | www.mcomd.org |
| Potomac A.T. Club | www.patc.net |
| Old Dominion A.T. Club | www.odatc.net |
| Tidewater A.T. Club | www.tidewateratc.com |
| Natural Bridge A.T. Club | www.nbatc.org |
| Roanoke A.T. Club | www.ratc.org |
| Outdoor Club at Virginia Tech | www.ocvt.club |
| Piedmont A.T. Hikers | www.piedmontathikers.org |
| Mount Rogers A.T. Club | www.mratc.org |
| Tennessee Eastman Hiking Club | www.tehcc.org |
| Carolina Mountain Club | www.carolinamountainclub.org |
| Smoky Mountains Hiking Club | www.smhclub.org |
| Nantahala Hiking Club | www.nantahalahikingclub.org |
| Georgia A.T. Club | www.georgia-atclub.org |

# Appalachian Trail Conservancy

Since 1925, the Appalachian Trail Conservancy (ATC) has been leading the management and conservation of the Appalachian Trail and its landscape—a sanctuary from the modern world where nature thrives and people can connect with its transformative power. Each year, the A.T. landscape draws millions of visitors, serves as a critical wildlife corridor and refuge for thousands of diverse species, and plays a vital role in driving climate resilience and economic vitality in neighboring communities.

As the only non-profit devoted exclusively to the entire Trail, ATC's dedicated team works passionately to bolster the health, resilience, and connectivity of the A.T. and its surrounding natural lands, manage the resources and grassroots effort needed to maintain the integrity of the treadway, and enrich visitor experiences by providing essential knowledge for safe and fulfilling Trail experiences.

In this vein, ATC has a wealth of resources on its website to help hikers plan their visits to the A.T. Resources include a Hiker Resource Library, Leave No Trace education, a free interactive map, hike registration, and the latest Trail updates, closures, and conditions.

The work of the ATC is not possible without its dedicated supporters and members. Consider joining today to support our work and help keep the Trail alive.

Learn more at appalachiantrail.org.

## HISTORY OF THE *APPALACHIAN TRAIL DATA BOOK*

The model for the *Appalachian Trail Data Book* was the "Mileage Fact Sheet" compiled by Ed Garvey and Gus Crews, published simultaneously in 1971 by the then-Appalachian Trail Conference and Appalachian Books (Oakton, Virginia) as an appendix to the late Mr. Garvey's *Appalachian Hiker*.

The first edition (1977) of the *Appalachian Trail Data Book* was compiled by the late Raymond F. Hunt of Kingsport, Tennessee, who continued to perform this volunteer service annually until 1983.

For over 40 years, the *Data Book* has been compiled by Daniel D. Chazin of Teaneck, New Jersey, an active volunteer with the New York–New Jersey Trail Conference and editor of the *Appalachian Trail Guide to New York–New Jersey*. Each fall he draws on the work of editors and data compilers of the other ten guidebooks, thirty maintaining Clubs, and Appalachian Trail Conservancy staff for updated information on each section of the Appalachian Trail.

# The Appalachian Trail Community™ Network

The Appalachian Trail Community™ program is an ATC initiative that seeks to develop mutually beneficial relationships with interested towns and counties along the Trail—to enhance their economies, further protect the Trail, and engage a new generation of volunteers.

Communities designated as of November 2025:

**Kingfield, ME**
**Millinocket, ME**
**Monson, ME**
**Rangeley, ME**
**Gorham, NH**
**Hanover, NH**
**Bennington, VT**
**Manchester, VT**
**Norwich, VT**
**Cheshire, MA**
**Dalton, MA**
**Great Barrington, MA**
**Lee, MA**
**North Adams, MA**
**Harlem Valley (Dover and Pawling), NY**
**Warwick, NY**
**Greater Blairstown, NJ**
**Vernon, NJ**
**Boiling Springs, PA**
**Delaware Water Gap, PA**
**Duncannon, PA**
**Greater Waynesboro, PA**
**Wind Gap, PA**
**Boonsboro, MD**
**Brunswick, MD**
**Harpers Ferry/Bolivar, WV**
**Abingdon, VA**
**Berryville/Clarke County, VA**
**Bland, VA**
**Bluemont, VA**
**Buena Vista, VA**
**Damascus, VA**
**Elkton, VA**
**Front Royal/Warren County, VA**
**Glasgow, VA**
**Harrisonburg, VA**
**Hillsboro, VA**
**Luray/Page County, VA**
**Marion/Smyth County, VA**
**Narrows, VA**
**Nelson County, VA**
**Pearisburg, VA**
**Troutville, VA**
**Round Hill, VA**
**Waynesboro, VA**
**Roan Mountain, TN**
**Unicoi County, TN**
**Fontana Dam, NC**
**Franklin, NC**
**Hot Springs, NC**
**Blairsville/Union County, GA**
**Clayton/Rabun County, GA**
**Dahlonega, GA**
**Ellijay/Gilmer County, GA**
**Hiawassee/Towns County, GA**
**Helen/White County, GA**

Those listed in the *Data Book* are indicated by a ★ in the Facilities column.

**MOUNTAINEERS BOOKS**, including its two imprints, Skipstone and Braided River, is a leading publisher of quality outdoor recreation, sustainability, and conservation titles. As a 501(c)(3) nonprofit, we are committed to supporting the environmental and educational goals of our organization by providing expert information on human-powered adventure, sustainable practices at home and on the trail, and preservation of wilderness.

Our publications are made possible through the generosity of donors, and through sales of 700 titles on outdoor recreation, sustainable lifestyle, and conservation. To donate, purchase books, or learn more, visit us online:

**MOUNTAINEERS BOOKS**
1001 SW Klickitat Way, Suite 201 • Seattle, WA 98134
800-553-4453 • mbooks@mountaineersbooks.org • mountaineersbooks.org

*An independent nonprofit publisher since 1960*

Mountaineers Books is proud to support the Leave No Trace Center for Outdoor Ethics, whose mission is to use the power of science, education, and stewardship to ensure a sustainable future for the outdoors and the planet. The Leave No Trace program is focused specifically on human-powered (nonmotorized) recreation. For more information, visit www.lnt.org.